INZANE

InZane

A D2S Publishing book
PO Box 745323
Arvada, CO 80006

Editor: Jane Dratz

Black, Zane.
InZane: Totally Stoked on this Jesus Dude
ISBN: 978-0-9827733-3-8
Library of Congress Control Number: 2011941066

Printed in the United States of America
1 2 3 4 5 6 7 8 9 / 12 11 10 09 08 07 06

Dedicated to all those people who have helped shape me into the person I am today.

Contents

Preface   iix

1. ME   8
2. HIGH School   14
3. Messed Up   20
4. Sin is Fun   28
5. Night of Horror   34
6. Radical Love: People and God   42
7. Up in Smoke   50
8. Rocked My World   58
9. All This and More   66
10. Take a Stand   72
11. ALL IN   80
12. Bros, Pros and Groms   92
13. Same Old Zane   104
14. LIT   118
15. THE Cause   126
16. In Zane   138

Prologue   146

Zane Slang   149

Preface

It is pretty funny that I am writing a book. Especially because it doesn't even have pop up pages or anything sweet like that. Donald Miller said in *A Million Miles in a Thousand Years* that this is where the author is supposed to apologize for where the book falls short. Well, I'm not apologizing, I mean let's be real here, although I am writing a book, it's still just me, Zane, or as my family called me growing up InZane. I didn't all of a sudden morph into super spiritual author man or something like that. My vocabulary still consists mainly of words like dude, legit, sick and yes, even RAD (a little blast from the '80s). So, this is me, like it or not, it's me. ☺ I don't know if you are allowed to put smiley faces in a book......but that just happened. ☺

Oh yeah, and for you old—I mean, more mature—people who might read this, there is a list of word definitions in the back, just in case you missed it that sick no longer has to do with having a cold. The words marked with the little * are the ones I'm giving you some help on.

CHAPTER 1

ME

My name is Zane Black... aaaannnnndddd I…...LOVE JESUS!

But that hasn't always been the case. For most of my life I wanted nothing to do with the dude. For 21 years of my life I lived for my own pleasures and desires.

I wanted to experience life, and life to the fullest. Maybe you can relate, you want to experience happiness, joy, excitement and fullness of life. I heard a statistic the other day, 10 out of 10 people…die. Yep, I haven't tested it yet, but I believe it is true. Which tells me that you and I got one life to live. We have got one shot at this thing. And I don't know about you, but I want to experience it to the fullest.

I have always been the type of guy to go all in as part of my quest to experience the most excitement and adventure

LOVIN' LIFE AND LOVIN' JESUS!

life has to offer. I just ended up "going all in" for the wrong things. For so much of my life, I tried to find happiness in all the wrong places and it almost cost me my life. Some people say it was that I got caught up in the wrong crowd, you know, peer pressure. I think it was that I was looking for a place to fit in, and it just so happened that the crowd who welcomed me in was the party crew. But I'm getting ahead of my story…

I was raised by parents who loved me and went to great lengths to give me the best life they knew how. I am so thankful for my mom and my dad, they are awesome people. Although they loved me, their love for each other didn't last because they got divorced by the time I was four years old. People often ask me if it was hard being raised in a broken home. Honestly, I don't know any different. I never remember my parents being together. The first time I ever saw my parents in the same place and getting along was when they both came to my college graduation and rented a car together. It was weird…but awesome.

I don't remember a ton from my childhood and growing up. It seems that my memories have been clouded by fermented

I STILL HAVE THAT HEADBAND...
AND I STILL WEAR IT!

LEARNIN' EARLY.

hops and bong resin. Some people say that drugs have no effect on you. Try telling your doctor that. Because of that stuff, most of my memories of the past are like looking over a valley covered in fog. I can make out most of it, but the details are hazy.

Well, no worries, I am not going to try to recount all the fuzzy details of my life to you here. Most of it, I would rather not share at all, since I wish I could totally forget a bunch of it myself. The stuff I'm telling you about in this book is all in hopes of helping you avoid my same mistakes.

MA & ME

APPARENTLY I THOUGHT I WAS TOUGH IN SPANDEX SHORTS. UNFORTUNATELY I LOOK LIKE I WAS STARVING.

INZANE

I'm going to try to share with you what formed me into the person I am today. I'm not doing this because I'm such a great guy and think that everyone should want to be like me. HECK NO! I'm doing it to show that no person is a lost cause. There is no one who has done too much or strayed too far from the outstretched hands of God's love and forgiveness. And once that love and forgiveness penetrates the walls of a person's heart, their potential becomes as vast as the stars in the sky. My life is proof.

A friend once said, "Thank God I am not the person I use to be, and thank God that He is not through making me into the person He wants me to be." I am not the same person I was years ago, but just because my life has been changed, it doesn't mean I've got it all together now either. God's not done yet, my story isn't finished and neither is yours. There is more to be written. I hope this book will encourage you and help you realize just how much adventure, fulfillment, joy and purpose is still to be experienced in the unwritten part of your story. If you allow God to be the author.

CHAPTER 2
HIGH SCHOOL

"So Zane, do you know why I called you into my office today?"

Side note: I don't even remember the principal's name, which is funny considering how much quality time he and I spent together in his office. Oh, the memories, like when I pulled the fire alarm so we could all get out of school early, or when my friends and I got busted for hot boxing my car (smoking weed until the entire car was full of smoke).

Back to the story—sorry my brain wanders, as you shall soon find out. I started thinking, "This is a trick question. This is where he wants me to start confessing the stuff I did that he doesn't know about. No way is he tricking me…this time."

"No, I can't imagine why I would be in here, I thought maybe you just missed having me in your office, so you invited me back to hang out," I said as seriously as possible, trying to sell it like a used car salesman, as though I really thought he wanted to hang out.

He was not impressed and I could tell he was cutting straight to the issue, but it was weird, because he didn't seem mad. He sort of sat back in his chair with a smirk on his face, a posture of confidence, and peered at me with this look of intensity, almost as if to say, "That's right, I've got you now."

GOT YOU NOW

He then began to speak in a low voice as he folded his hands and looked at the ground. "It appears that you have missed a lot of classes this year, unexcused absences. My guess is that you were skipping class," he paused, "although I can't exactly prove it."

Of course he couldn't prove it. I had figured out the system. I could miss one class every day without the automatic caller dialing my house. Sure, there were some close calls, like the time I almost got caught and ended up getting chased by the rent-a-cop through the woods as I was leaving campus. I can still remember him shouting over his walkie talkie, "I got Zane in my sight and he is on the run!" But they never caught me; rent-a-cop spent too much time eating twinkies and not enough time on the treadmill. And since he didn't catch me, they couldn't prove it was me.

The principal continued, "But it looks like I don't have to prove it. You have missed so many classes that state law says I don't have to let you graduate."

Those words echoed over and over in my head. Now he had my attention, and I began to squirm in my seat. He let the moment just hang there in awkward silence. Finally he added, "If I don't let you graduate, then you've got another year here...but I've been thinking,"

My heart stopped, I felt as though my whole high school career flashed before my eyes. Fun memories, but I was not digging the idea of round two.

He continued, "But I don't want you back for another year, so I'm going to let you graduate."

I about flew out of my chair and kissed the old dude as I shouted, "Looks like we finally agree on something, I'm outta here!"

Now looking back, I realize that I was a punk kid, who wasted much of my life trying to figure out who I really am.

You see, I hadn't made the best choices in my teenage years. In the 6th grade I started drinking, in the 7th grade I started smoking and by the 9th grade I started doing drugs. I realized pretty quickly that drugs ain't cheap, so I started selling drugs to pay for my own habits. I sold drugs through my junior and senior year in high school, and then got fully wrapped up in it after high school. I made a ton of money, but lost a ton of brain cells. My theory was that I had billions of brain cells and so I could afford to lose a few....guess I was wrong.

My lack of brain cells caused me to make even more poor decisions, some of which would have consequences that would stick with me for the rest of my life. I ended up getting involved sexually with girls and lost my virginity when I was in 9th grade. I realized later in life that was something I could never get back.

Our decisions affect not only us, but others as well. I found this out years later when I had to tell my future wife that I had given away something that was so special and meant

I'M REALLY EXCITED ABOUT WHATEVER I AM EATING!

for marriage to somebody else. All of our decisions have consequences, and some consequences last a lifetime.

If you have made the same horrible decisions I made, then you know what I'm talking about, or you soon will, because it's only a matter of time before the consequences of your decisions catch up with you. Maybe you haven't made as bad of decisions as I have; that's good, but know that even the bad choices that seem insignificant can still have really bad, long lasting outcomes. Many of the choices we make, we can't go back on. That's what happened to me, as you'll soon see.

Don't get me wrong, I had a ton of fun growing up. I hope you are living it up as a teenager, too. I mean, your teenage years have the potential to be some of the best years of your life. I know school can be boring and it's kind of embarrassing going through puberty, but think about it, someday you are going to have to work for a living. Some of you will even have to start cooking food for yourself and doing laundry for the first time of your life—real responsibility.

So you got to make the most of these teenage years. You got one shot at being a teenager and there is no going back. And I want to help you get the most out of these next years in life so you can look back with no regrets.

CHAPTER 3
MESSED UP

Shortly after graduation I ended up leaving the house because of my relationship with my step mom. And I moved in with my girlfriend—another poor decision. I had lived with my dad and step mom since the 6th grade and I didn't always get along the best with my step mom, which probably had more to do with me than it did with her. We fought a lot and my dad worked hard to provide for the family, so he often worked late. I found myself feeling all alone.

At first when I moved out, I thought it was great—freedom at last! I was 18 years old and on my own. I ended up getting a job at a beer company (so I got tons of free beer). I also ended up moving in with the girl I thought I loved.

The reality of my poor lifestyle choices came crashing down on me the night my girlfriend told me she was pregnant. I was still in my teens, how could I raise a child? I was stuck with one of the toughest decisions in my life, and it left me feeling like I had nowhere to turn. I became fearful of what people would think of me, how my life would change, what I would miss out on, and how to protect myself. All of my reasoning was focused on me.

So I made the decision for my girlfriend to have an abortion. Even as I write that word I feel sick, nauseous. As though time slows down, leaving me in a place of emptiness.

You know, you make a lot of decisions in life, little ones, big ones, but some decisions you will never forget.

There will be decisions that you make that stick with you for the rest of your life. I have carried the weight of that decision around with me ever since, like a backpack filled with rocks. Every time I talk about it, I feel as though a little part of me breaks. It has been over 10 years, and still sometimes I break down, losing all control of my emotions and I weep. I know now that I am forgiven, but that awful decision will never be forgotten.

When I look back over my life, there are a lot of things that I am ashamed of, but I realized those are the events that make me who I am today. Although I am not proud of many of the decisions I have made, and this one decision more than any I wish I could go back on, I believe God has used some of these stupid choices to shape me.

Here is what I mean. When I was 21, I was invited to a friend's church (which I will talk more about later). I was looking for answers. At that church I heard verses like Romans 3:23: "For all have sinned and fall short of the glory of God." Which means that everyone is messed up. For me, that was good news, because it meant that I wasn't alone, we ALL have sinned. It can be easy to look at my life and see that I was messed up, no doubt about it, I am a sinner. My sin was so glaringly obvious that I couldn't miss it. But not everybody realizes the depth of their sin.

Often we like to set standards, we look at our own lives and then measure what it is to be good based on us as the standard. When we are the ones defining what's good and bad, we always end up on the good side, not like super "Mother Teresa" good, but good enough to make it. To make sure we aren't really bad, we often judge by how bad others are. I sometimes find myself judging how good I am compared to how bad others are. The problem is I usually have to compare myself to people like "axe murderers" and "bank robbers." I guess it makes me feel better, because "at least I am not as bad as they are."

GOOD

EVIL

AXE MURDERER ZANE BLACK MOTHER TERESA

The problem is, God says, "*No one is good—except God alone*" (Mark 10:18). God also says that the standard we must measure ourselves against is His perfection. "*Be perfect, therefore, as your heavenly Father is perfect*" (Matthew 5:48). In light of that standard, we all fall short and we are all in desperate need of help.

So in comparing myself to an "axe murderer," I am looking in the wrong direction. I am looking outward to other people when I should be looking upward to God and then inward at myself.

Hatred in His Eyes

I had just finished speaking at a Dare 2 Share conferences when a student approached me and asked if we could chat. I was so stoked, because I always love the chance to get to know as many Dare 2 Share conference students as possible. As we began to chat, it was clear that there was something really bothering this guy.

Then he dropped the bomb, "When I came to this conference last year you were my hero. I saw how you lived for God and I wanted that for myself. Then you shared about how you and your girlfriend got an abortion. Ever since then, I have hated you. How could you have done such a thing?"

This kid was ticked, I could see the hatred in his eyes. I don't know what came over me, and this has never happened before or since. I usually try and be more caring, but not this time. I looked directly into this guy's eyes and said, "You know man, I think that God also was angry about my sin, and that it affected Him, too. But you know what? Jesus says that if you hate a person, then it is the same as murdering them. You see, Jesus equates hate and murder. You hate me because I murdered an innocent child. Well, guess what, your hate is just as evil in God's eyes. So guess what, man, you and I, we're in the same boat...murderers."

The Bible says, "*Whoever keeps the whole law and yet stumbles at just one point is guilty of breaking all of it*" (James 2:10). It doesn't matter if your list of sins could fill an entire library, or if your list could fit on a little sticky note. It doesn't even matter if all you ever did was steal a pen or disrespect your parents, (we have all blown that one!). We are sinners. So regardless of how good or bad you feel you are, we are all in the same boat—sinners, broken, we've missed the mark, we've fallen short. Romans 6:23

says, "*the wages of sin*"—what we earn for falling short—"*is death.*" You and I both have earned death. We have been separated from true life, even separated from the ability to experience the fullness of life.

This is one of the key ingredients to the Christian life... knowing your need...realizing your sin...acknowledging your failures. Because it shows that you have need, need of someone to save you, a "SAVIOR." Many of us would acknowledge that we have sinned, but do we realize the full severity of our sin? If you never acknowledge the magnitude of your mess ups, you most likely will miss the fullness of forgiveness. Derek Webb says it this way: "You will be a hypothetical sinner, with a hypothetical Savior."

Why do I tell you this? In the hope that you will catch downwind of your sin and that you will be repulsed by it. And in the same breath you will smell the sweet aroma of the sacrifice Jesus made on your behalf, and it will cause you to look to Him for forgiveness, love, life and freedom.

As one of my good friends and mentors, Derwin Gray, says, "Marinate on this."

Another good friend, Jesus, says, "*He who has been forgiven little, loves little*" (Luke 7:47).

CHAPTER 4
SIN
IS FUN

I remember the first time I spoke at a youth group after I became a Christian, because the look on their faces is forever imprinted in my memory. I wish you could have seen it. I had gotten through telling my story of all the horrible stuff that I put myself and others through, and I mean, I told it all, holding nothing back. It was a pretty intense moment, to say the least. I could sense that the students, chaperons and leaders were really taken aback with how honest I was, with the magnitude of my sin and its consequences in my life. Until I said this: "I am going to say something that may offend some of you." I paused and let it sink in a little bit, and then very slowly with extra volume I put it out there straight and clear: "SIN IS FUN!" Eyes got as big as saucers, mouths literally dropped open.

One of the male adult sponsors looked like he was about to rush the stage and take me out!

It's true, sin is fun…in the moment. The drugs, the alcohol, the parties, the girls, it was all fun. Maybe right now you are blown away that I am saying this. But think about it, if it wasn't fun, people wouldn't do it. People don't go to parties thinking, "I can't wait till I get really drunk and say stupid things that friends will tease me about later, and maybe I'll get really drunk and puke on myself in front of a real cute girl." Or, "I can't wait till the hangover, I just love that feeling in the morning where my head feels like it was hit with a sledge hammer, my whole body feels like I was hit by a freight train and my mouth tastes like someone POOPED in it."

THIS FACE SAYS IT ALL!

No! People do it because at the time it seems fun, and it is. The Bible even recognizes that sin is fun. Hebrews 11:25 describes Moses as "*choosing rather to be mistreated with the people of God than to enjoy the fleeting **pleasures** of sin*" (ESV). If you are honest, at some level, you too have enjoyed the pleasures of sin. I don't just mean the drinkin' and the druggin' type of sin, but any sin. Because all sin entices us by claiming to bring fulfillment or joy, but always fails to deliver in the end. But like the Bible says, you have also probably found those pleasures to be fleeting. Or as the King James Version of the Bible puts it, the pleasures only last "*for a season*."

It's like jumping off a building without a parachute. The first 100 feet is gonna be epic.* But when the reality of the ground comes, you will find your epic free fall to have been short lived, with a terrible ending. In my free fall of sin, I began to catch glimpses of the quickly approaching pavement.

But not only did I find the pleasures of sin faded away like a snowball in a hot tub, I also started experiencing the horrible side effects of my stupid choices. After the abortion, my girlfriend and I broke up and my life really started spinning out of control. I was selling drugs, people were always calling me for the hookup,* so I had a ton of friends, I had money, could throw raging parties and I was dating multiple girls at once, thinking I was the man. It was weird though, because although I felt like I had everything that I thought would make me happy, I was often left empty.

All over the world people chase after the pleasures of this world, seeking their own desires and end up being left

31

unsatisfied. One of the top snowboarders in the world is Shaun White. Shaun turned pro at the age of 13. He has won over 24 medals through competition and has his own clothing brand and snowboard outerwear line. He has a video game made after him. Red Bull built him his own personal half pipe in the mountains of Colorado. They estimate he makes around $9 million a year!

The show *60 Minutes* did a story on Shaun and in the interview he said something shocking. He put it out there straight up and said, "I'm a bit lonely sometimes." He's gotten to the top of his career, is living out every shred* kid's dreams, is traveling the world, snowboarding and skateboarding for a living, and yet he is lonely.

John Mayer, a well known musician, has 3.7 million Twitter followers and 2.3 million Facebook fans, yet he has a song where he sings about all that he has in the form of a checklist: "Friends- check, money- check, well slept- check, opposite sex- check...." He goes on, but the chorus of the song is "something's missing and I don't know how to fix it, something's missing and I don't know what it is."

Why is it that people all over the world are seeking for life & satisfaction, yet they miss it?

I was the same way, though. I could find nothing that fully satisfied.

What started as experimenting with drugs and alcohol turned into a full on indulgence that left me continually longing for more. Those sensations I felt when I first got drunk or high were fleeting; my attempts to escape from reality increasingly required more substances to get that same feeling I'd once had.

My life began to spin out of control in a downward spiral of my own indulgences. What started as something I would do for fun began ruining the very life I was trying to experience.

"If I find in myself a desire which no experience in this world can satisfy, the most probable explanation is that I was made for another world." — C.S. Lewis

CHAPTER 5
NIGHT
OF HORROR

Even friends began to see that my life was getting out of control. At one point, some friends tried to talk sense into me, to get me to slow down. But that was like the blind leading the blind, seeing as most of my friends were just as lost and caught up in the scene as I was. Regardless, I knew there was some validity to my life getting out of control, I just didn't know what the solution was. I ended up trying to quit doing drugs, but it turned out I needed something to fill the void, so I would get drunk instead.

One night specifically, I was out with a friend to go see a movie and we decided to get wasted first. He decided to get high and my way of resisting the temptation to smoke weed was to drink more. I ended up drinking an entire bottle of vodka and started getting belligerent. By the time we got to the movies, I was fully out of control.

During the first 10 minutes of the movie, my friend told me (I don't remember) that I started yelling at the movie, making a fool of myself. Then I made a break for the bathroom. My buddy noticed I'd been gone a while, so he came to check on me. He found me halfway conscious locked in the bathroom stall. He figured I would be all right, so he left. But little did he know I was moments away from passing out in the stall.

Luckily, a movie theater custodian found me unconscious, laying on the bathroom floor and called 911. Apparently, when the EMTs tried to rescue me I got violent and tried to fight them; I wasn't much of a match considering my condition. During the scuffle I passed out again, and this time I wasn't coming back around.

My body slipped into a coma because of all the alcohol I had consumed. You see, the problem with alcohol is that when you drink large amounts, it acts like a lethal poison. Because I drank so much, the alcohol began to shut down my vital organs one by one. They rushed me to the hospital and began to pump my stomach to try and get the alcohol out before it killed me.

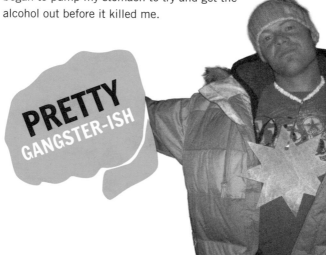

PRETTY GANGSTER-ISH

The hospital contacted my mom and she had to come and see her baby boy on his death bed. The doctors told my mom that I might not make it through the night. And if I did survive, I could be in a coma for the rest of my life. Or if I came out of the coma, I may have brain damage and never be the same person ever again.

Surprise!!! If you didn't figure it out, I made it, I'm alive. The brain damage is debatable, but I survived.

You would think that after all of that I would have gotten my life together. I didn't. I continued to fall even deeper into the pit of despair, feeling like my only escape was to continue in this lifestyle of partying, drinking and getting even more involved in the drug scene. I couldn't quit, so I decided I might as well give in.

Really, I was looking to find life, joy and happiness. I just didn't look in the best places.

But in my quest for finding life, trying to experience life to the fullest, I almost lost my life.

Blaise Pascal once said, "There is a God shaped vacuum in the heart of every man which cannot be filled by any created thing, but only by God, the Creator, made known through Jesus." I believe it, because I lived it. By the time I was 21, I had tried so many things, each of them ending like a bad movie. You know those movies that keep you entertained just enough to keep you watching and then end horribly, leaving you feeling like you wasted two hours of your life that you'll never get back. Well, I felt like I'd wasted years.

Jesus says in John 10:10, "*The thief comes only to steal and kill and destroy; I have come that they may have life, and have it to the full.*" I don't know what you think about demons or the devil, but the reality is there is something that is out to destroy your life. Jesus calls that evil something Satan—"the thief." Satan hates you and wants the worst for you. He wants your life to end like a bad movie.

But God also says that the reason Jesus came was to offer us life—true, real and abundant life! This life is available to you

and me, and it comes through a relationship, through getting to know God. Jesus later explains how we enter into this life when He says, "*This is eternal life*"—which by the way is not just a length of life, but a quality of life—"*this is eternal life, that they may know you, the only true God, and Jesus Christ, whom you have sent*" (John 17:3).

Baaaaam! That's it! Life is found in knowing Jesus. Not in how much you go to church, whether or not you were raised in a Christian home, how much you read your Bible or how little or much you sin, but in KNOWING JESUS!

For so long I missed it. I was deceived by the one who was seeking to destroy my life, I was looking for life and happiness in all the wrong places. I was more than "lost," I was headed for destruction. Jesus says there is a way out. Everything that I was looking for—acceptance, adventure and fun—can actually be found in knowing Jesus! If there really is a God who created this world, then fun is from Him, it was His idea, and He is the one who knows how to experience the fullness of it.

◀ ONE OF MY FAVORITE WAYS
TO SPEND **AN AFTERNOON!**

39

What about you? Where are you looking to find satisfaction, happiness, life and joy?

It's not just the druggies like me that miss that "life to the full" that we were meant to experience. So many people look to the wrong places to find life. People look to money, fame, education, sports, friends, family and all sorts of things that aren't bad, but they were never meant to fully satisfy. Jesus alone was meant to give us true satisfaction, life to the fullest, real happiness and abundant joy.

In Matthew 5:6 Jesus says, "*Blessed are those who hunger and thirst for righteousness, for they shall be satisfied*" (ESV). Jesus says that true life and satisfaction come only in Him, getting to know Him, living for Him, because this is the purpose you were made for.

A friend, an ex-stoner turned Jesus freak, once said, "Put THAT in your theological pipe and smoke it." Which is another way of saying, think about it.

CHAPTER 6
RADICAL LOVE:
PEOPLE AND GOD

Shortly after the overdose and the abortion, I really began to question the meaning of life. Like, why are we all here?

I had wasted two years after high school doing my own thing. The whole drug dealing was getting old, and although I liked all the free beer, I wasn't sure I wanted to be a beer delivery guy for the rest of my life. I'm not trashing beer delivery guys, I mean, I also don't want to be a rocket scientist either, and supposedly they are the standard by which we judge smart people. I just didn't think delivering beer was what I wanted to be doing for the long haul. So I decided I would go to college. Ha!

I ended up moving back home with my dad and step mom so I could afford college. Plus, macaroni and cheese with hot dogs was getting pretty old (I know you think it's good now, but wait till you eat it every day, breakfast, lunch and dinner, you wait and see). I started taking classes at the community college, still working at the beer company and selling drugs on the side.

Well, that lasted a couple months and then I came home one night and as I opened the door, I saw my step mom sitting on the stairs in the entry way, wrapped in a blanket, staring down at the steps. I slowly moved towards her to ask if everything was okay. As she looked up, I could see the mascara that had run down her face from the tears that had been streaming. Through her tears she said, "He's gone... He's gone."

"What?" I exclaimed, almost as a statement rather than a question, with fear and frustration in my voice.

"He's gone, he left me, your dad left," she said, her head collapsing into her arms, completely defeated.

I felt a sigh of relief at first, because initially I thought that maybe someone had died. But then I realized the weight of what just happened.

MY SIS AND I HAVE A SPECIAL BOND.

The next day I heard from my dad. Apparently things had gotten real difficult between them and it was over. My dad said this is what needed to happen. My dad's birthday was right around the corner and he said he wanted to meet me for dinner. I remember going to see my dad on his birthday at the restaurant. I had gotten him a skateboard for his b-day because I thought maybe it would be a good time to freshen up on his old skills. Plus, chicks dig skaters and Dad was single now.

We had a great time, it was so good to see him and he did seem happy, which was something I hadn't seen in a while. But there was something that seemed to be missing and I wondered if he really did miss my step mom, I mean they had been together 16 years.

Well, things got weird with me living with my dad's ex-wife, my ex-step mom (or however you would say that). I ended up leaving the house and moving in with my friend's parents. What they didn't know was that I was selling drugs to their kids. But this family just welcomed me in and they loved me.

Now my own parents have always loved me and gone to great lengths to show that love, and they did a great job at it. But sometimes as a kid, you kinda feel like the reason why your parents love you is because they are supposed to. You don't always realize just how much they do care until you get older, look back and see all that they sacrificed for you. But this family I'd moved in with was different. They didn't have to love me, but they did.

I am pretty sure the mom of the family knew about most of the partying and drugs. She for sure didn't know that I was selling, but there was a time or two she busted me for being high. I remember times when I would walk in the door and she would be like, "WOW!!!! Zane, can you even see out your eyes?...I bet you've got some serious munchies." I had given up on trying to hide my secrets and had gotten to the point where I didn't care if people knew about the drugs. But then she would sit me down and fix me some food. I remember one time when I was heading from one party to the next, had been drinking and driving and stopped by to get something. She tricked me into staying awhile with a nice home cooked

I LOVE
MY MOM

meal, which sobered me up and I ended up passing out on the couch. Their love for me was subtle, but effective.

Then a day came when the mom put the effects of their love to the test. She invited me to church. I thought she was crazy! I didn't belong in church; I would probably get struck by lightning just for walking into the place. What was she thinking? But I trusted her, so I went.

Looking back I realized the sacrifice and effort that family made for me. They loved me with a radical love, and it worked. It was their love, which was really the love of God, that began to chisel away at my hard heart. They never told me what I was doing was wrong (even though it was wrong). I guess they figured I already knew the stuff I was doing was wrong. Which was true and is true for most—deep down most people have a conscience that tells them there's something wrong with their selfish, sinful ways. I didn't need someone to tell me I was making poor choices; I needed someone to show me a different choice.

Think of it this way. If there was a poisonous tree in my backyard that I wanted to get rid of, I would not try to kill it by pulling off all the leaves one by one. I would get to the root, or to the trunk, and then cut it down or root it up. The leaves are just an outgrowth of what's happening at the root. Same in life, the sin in our life is just an outgrowth of what's happening at the root. The problem is not that we do bad things; it's that at the core there's a problem. By nature we are sinful and selfish, which is why you never have to teach a toddler to be selfish, they're born like that.

This family seemed to understand this truth and they didn't judge me. They loved me and in doing so, they lived out the gospel. They showed me that God accepts us as we are. No matter how bad you have been or the horrible things you have done, God loves you. He wants to show you another way. Christianity is NOT a message of clean yourself up before you come to God. I couldn't change on my own; I had tried to quit the drugs before and ended up in a coma, almost losing my life. God wants us to come to Him as we are, and then He promises He will give us the strength to overcome our struggles. He alone has the power to change us from the inside out.

God is not some angry dude up in the clouds waiting to blast you for all the junk you've done. His heart breaks, knowing the hurt and pain that you go through trying to live this life separated from a relationship with Him. He is extending His hand to you right now, to reach you with the reality of His love. He knows the depth of your pain, the difficulty of your struggles, and He wants to help. This is why He sent His one and only Son, Jesus, to die, to experience the punishment for your sin and to express the fullness of His love for you as you are.

But it takes you experiencing God's radical love for YOU. His love can be experienced in many different ways. It may come from other Christians as they live out God's love, it can come as we read God's Word and hear His words of love for us and it can even come as we get away from all other distractions and just talk to God in the quiet. This is where my words fall short. You need to hear the words of your Father in heaven who is longing for His child to return home.

The love of God the Father is expressed through Jesus in Luke 19 when Zacchaeus, a sinful man, experiences the radical love of Jesus even though Zacchaeus is still in the midst of his sin. It is the radical love of God that pierces his heart, and changes his life. Grab a Bible and spend a little time here exploring it for yourself.

READ IT

Luke 19: 1-10. Zacchaeus was stuck in his sin. But Jesus went to Zacchaeus' house (which is equivalent to accepting someone as your friend) and Zacchaeus was changed by the radical love of Jesus.

LIVE IT

1. Have you experienced that radical, life-changing love of God?
2. If so, then what does it look like for you to love and accept others with that same love?
3. If not, read on.

49

CHAPTER 7
UP IN SMOKE

Walking through the large wooden doors of the church with my friend's mom (the mom of the kids I was selling drugs to) gave me a feeling like I didn't belong. These people had it all together, or at least they made it look like they had it all together. They were all dressed nice, smiles on their faces, Bibles in hand. Sure some of them could have been faking it, but let's be honest, I was beyond the point of faking like I had anything together. So I went just as I was, which meant with a hangover from the night before.

I don't remember anything that pastor dude said while I was there, but during my day dreaming and doodling, I spotted this on the little pamphlet they gave out: "If you're a first time visitor COME BY THE WELCOME CENTER FOR A FREE GIFT." I never knew! I could do this every Sunday, visit a new church and get tons of free gifts!

So I walked over to the Welcome Center, presented my little pamphlet and then waited in anticipation. I was thinking "it's a hot summer day, maybe I'll get a Popsicle or something sweet like that." As I was lost in lala land thinking about how cool my free gift was going to be, I got interrupted by the welcome center lady who said, "Would you like the NIV or the King James," as she held out these two paperback Bibles.

INZANE

My first thought…"You would! Trick me with the hopes of
some free gift, lure me in with the thought of a nice Popsicle
on a hot day and then give me a Bible! What's up with that?"

Turns out the lady was pretty persistent and I ended up
walking away with the dang thing. Now I have had Bibles
before, I mean, every good American has at least a couple
copies collecting dust somewhere in the house. It is the
world's best seller, after all—I know you thought *Harry Potter*
or *Twilight* was, so sorry to rain on your parade—but the
Bible is the all time best seller. Some dude in a suit riding a
bike gave me a Bible one time when I was in high school. I
ended up using the thin papers to roll a joint and smoked it.
I took the rest and used it to light a bonfire. See, I told you I
felt like I was going to get struck by lightning when I walked
through the doors of that church.

I just heard a story recently about a pastor who would go out
on the streets and hand out Bibles to people just passing
by. One day he was talking with a homeless dude trying to
tell him about Jesus, but all the homeless dude wanted was
something to roll a joint with. So the preacher guy made a
deal with homeless dude and said, "I will give you this Bible.
You can use the pages to roll your joint, but you have to
promise me that you will read every page before you smoke
it." So the homeless dude agreed to the preacher guy's rules.

A couple years later, the preacher is getting done preaching a Sunday sermon at his church and this dude comes up to him and says, "Remember me?" Pastor guy has no clue who this dude is and the dude says, "You gave me a Bible a couple years ago." Pastor guy thinks, oh how cool, I give a lot of Bibles away. But this wasn't just any old Bible giveaway and the dude went on to explain. "I was homeless and was trying to find papers to roll a joint." Pastor guy remembers right away. Dude goes on, "You said I had to read every page I smoked. Well, I smoked Mark, I smoked Matthew, I smoked Luke, but John smoked me!" Turns out the homeless dude read…and smoked his way through all the gospels and God spoke through the words on the page to change this dude's life.

START IN THE BOOK OF JOHN.

So I wasn't the only one who smoked a little Bible.

Anyway, back to my story. As I was walking away, Bible in hand, the lady shouted at me, "We recommend that new believers start reading in the book of John." Now I am a little confused. This lady has now called this the NIV, the Bible and now something about reading John. Maybe she said a good place to read is on the john? Whatever. As I walked out the door, this old dude stops me.

53

"How you doin', young man?" Remember, I was a punk kid at this time, and I would just say the first thing that came to my brain, which wasn't always good. My dad says that I have diarrhea of the mouth and constipation of the brain. So I responded, "Do you really care, or are you just asking to be polite?" I realized what I'd just said, but before I had a chance to take it back, the old dude busted out laughing. So I started laughing too and we ended up having a cool conversation. During the conversation the old dude pointed at the Bible in my hand and said, "Have you ever read it?"

WHEN YOU NO LONGER LIVE NEXT TO THE OCEAN, YOU GOTTA MAKE YOUR OWN SURF!

"Nope, and I wasn't really planning on it." I thought about telling him I had smoked one before, but figured I had already proved I was a punk.

Then he said something that I will never forget, and I am not sure if it was the way he said it or what, but it changed me forever. "Did you know if you read the Bible for about 15 minutes every day you could read the whole thing in one year?"

It was as if his words repeated in my head, but more as a challenge than a question. I realized that I didn't believe everything that I heard in church that day. I had a lot of questions, questions that needed answering. I knew my life wasn't turning out the way I wanted, but I wasn't just going to accept what some pastor said. Especially one who didn't know what I'd been through, but thought he had the answers to my problems. But I did wonder if there was more to life than just living for the now, more than parties and girls. I mean what if they are right? I am not a guy who will just take people's word for it, I usually have to try it myself.

So I decided right there and then that I was going to read the Bible, 15 minutes a day. I figured I had already experienced living my life for myself and it hadn't worked out so well.

What if there really was purpose in living a life for God?

As I walked away, the old dude also recommended that I start reading in the book of John. I didn't stop to tell him that I had no clue what he was talking about, I just nodded my head like any person would do who is totally confused, but doesn't want to make a fool of themselves.

CHAPTER 8
ROCKED
MY
WORLD

That night I got home…got high and then opened up the Bible. I realized quickly I had no clue what I was doing. It looked like there were different books within the Bible. It wasn't until like three-quarters of the way through the Bible that I found the book of John. I started thinking, "Why did everybody want me to start reading in John? I have gone to school a couple times and I learned enough to find out you start books in the beginning. What's in the beginning of this thing that they didn't want me to find out?"

Well, rather than start in John, I started in the beginning. Man did it ROCK MY WORLD! First, God creates the heavens, the earth and everything in it. Which sounded alright to me, because life is way too complex to have started by random chance (take girls for example…complex! ☺). Then God creates Adam and Eve, I'll give Him the credit because I don't feel like a monkey. Then Adam and Eve had kids, Cain and Abel, and Cain kills Abel! I freaked out, because I thought God's people were supposed to be perfect. Not so much. But that is not the craziest part, the Bible then says that the whole world became populated from this one family. Where I come from, we have a word for that.

The next Sunday I couldn't wait to go to church, because pastor dude had some explaining to do. I sat there not hearing a word; all I could think about were the questions I was going to ask. Soon as he got done and walked off stage I walked up to him with a few statements of my own aimed at proving Christianity wrong, "Homeboy, check it out, you guys believe..." and I finished with a whole list of questions, again trying to show that this whole Christianity thing didn't make sense. I can see it as if it was yesterday, he leaned his head slightly back, placing his hand under his chin as if to ponder what I said, and then spoke with a thoughtful look and a half smile, "Wow, I don't know."

"Wait, you don't know!" I shouted. "You run this place and you don't know?" I began thinking about the repercussions of this. I was about to announce to the entire church that they could go home, because pastor dude didn't know what he was talking about. But he interrupted with confidence and began to speak about Jesus, not in an arrogant way as if to shut me down. But in a bold confident way, as if to say, "my faith in Jesus doesn't depend on me understanding everything." I realized the Jesus he was talking about was not just theory. For pastor guy, Jesus was a real dude.

This wasn't the cardboard cut-out Jesus, or the Jesus in the picture frame, or the Jesus that only comes out at Christmas. He spoke about Jesus like He was his best friend, a real person, not just some make believe person. The pastor went on about how it was okay to have questions and that

even he had questions. Then he held up his Bible that looked like it had been through war because it was so well used, beat up, worn out, and hanging together by what looked like threads and said confidently, "The answers are in here."

I continued to read the Bible. Little by little, my life began to change. I began to realize there were things in my life that weren't right. I would learn things from the Bible and try to change the way I lived, based on what it said. Every night, I would read, I actually began to be excited about reading as I anticipated what new things I would learn as I adventured through the amazing stories I never knew existed. But there was something going on in my reading, and it was more than just entertainment from cool stories.

Hebrews 4:12-13 says:

For the word of God is living and active. Sharper than any double-edged sword, it penetrates even to dividing soul and spirit, joints and marrow; it judges the thoughts and attitudes of the heart. Nothing in all creation is hidden from God's sight. Everything is uncovered and laid bare before the eyes of him to whom we must give account.

It was like God was using the words on the pages to reach down to the very depths of my heart, causing me to rethink my way of life. I don't mean just rethink my bad decisions, but rethink everything. It was like the Bible was cutting straight through the walls I had built up, and I began to see the true depths of my need, pain and brokenness. In the same breath, I also felt there was hope, and I even began to experience comfort as I felt like my life was being "laid bare before Him."

Reading the Bible became more then just a chore, accomplishing the "read 15 minutes of the Bible" daily checklist. I began to crave it. The words on the pages would comfort me, speaking to my needs, and bring answers to my many questions. The words seemed to be far more than just words.

Did you know that the Bible actually claims to be "God breathed," the very words of God to us (2 Timothy 3:16)?

Although technically written by about 40 authors, it was as though the authors *"spoke from God as they were carried along by the Holy Spirit"* (2 Peter 1:21). Did you know you have access to the very words of God, and they could be sitting on your shelf collecting dust?

A Pretty Crazy Book

I found out later, the Bible is composed of 66 different books, written by like 40 different authors, in three different languages, from three different continents, compiled over a period of 1,500 years. Which makes it a pretty crazy book, considering it talks about hundreds, if not thousands, of subjects and not one part disagrees with another.

In the midst of our troubles we often run to so many different things for help. What if the comfort we are seeking and the answers we are looking for are closer than we ever knew. I am not saying that reading the Bible will make your life perfect. But I do know that God desires to meet your needs, bring you joy, comfort your pain and help you through the rough spots in life. And one of the ways He wants to do it is through His Word.

I challenge you...15 minutes a day. Start tonight. Some people like to get up early and read, that's okay too, but I like reading right before I go to bed. Otherwise, I just like the snooze button too much, but I don't mind staying up late. I hope you get in trouble for staying up late (because you were reading your Bible). Read two or three chapters and underline something that sticks out to you. You can think about that verse you underlined, journal about it or even memorize it. You can find a bunch of different Bible reading plan options to help you at www.biblegateway.com/resources/readingplans/. Start small, but start today. Oh yeah, and I really would start in the book of John.

Go eat a big fat steak (or veggie burger) and think about what Jesus said, "*Man does not live on bread alone, but on every word that comes from the mouth of God*" (Matthew 4:4).

Some of us Christians are starving to death; God wants us to feast.

Feast on His Word.

P.S. I have continued reading 15 minutes a day. I skip days, get behind, I'm actually like two weeks behind right now. But I have read the Bible all the way through nine times, one time for every year I have been a Christian. Which really isn't such a big deal; all it took was 15 minutes per day. And if you struggle reading, check out the audio Bibles. Maybe listen to it before you go to bed. For about a year I thought if I slept while listening to the Bible on my iPod, I would at least retain some of it. Every night I listened to about eight hours, until one night when I woke up as I was getting strangled by my headphone cord. So maybe listen for a bit before you fall asleep.

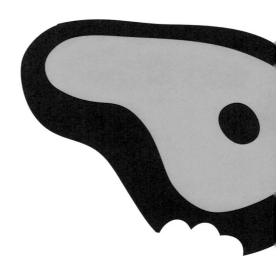

CHAPTER 9
ALL THIS
AND
MORE

I was driving home from one of the best days shreddin' that I'd had in a while. Life was good, I was going to church, reading a little Bible, which made me feel real sophisticated when people would come over to buy drugs and right next to a giant bag of weed would be my Bible. I was jamming to tunes, flying down the highway in the white Ford Explorer that I had just bought with drug money, feeling on top of the world. Little did I know it was all about to change forever.

I was interrupted by the sound of metal grinding, followed by smoke pouring out from underneath the hood. Next thing I knew I was cursing the car and God as I pounded the dash in complete anger at my broken down rig. About an hour later, I got picked up by a friend and left the truck on the side of the road. That night I was ticked. Is this what I get for trying to be a good guy, reading my Bible and going to church? Thanks a lot, God. So I decided it was back to the old Zane. We threw a little party at the house I was staying at and I was back to living as if I didn't care about a thing.

I was supposed to go teach snowboarding lessons the next day at a place called Crystal Mountain. But I had given

LEARNING TO SNOWBOARD.
SWEET GRAB!

up all hopes of that, until the craziest thing I had every experienced happened. I had just got done smoking some weed, beer in hand, and I walked outside to smoke a cigarette. As I opened the door and the fresh air hit me, my mind went blank and in a flash everything went black and then back to normal. All the way back to normal, as in, I was sober. Half freaked out and a little suspicious, I thought, "Well, that's never happened before."

I have never been a person who claims to have "heard from God," and it actually freaks me out a little when people say, "God told me_____." Maybe He has tried to speak to me audibly and I just have the music turned up too loud or something, but I have never heard His audible voice. I do wonder what He would sound like though, I bet He has an American accent. ☺ Anyway, that night it was like God "spoke" to my heart. I know it sounds weird, and it is really hard to explain, but it was like He began to place desires within my heart and I knew they weren't from me.

The Desires of Our Hearts

Psalm 37:4 says, *"Delight yourself in the Lord, and he will give you the desires of your heart."* God can give us the desires in our heart, or He can change the current desires we have and make them godly desires.

In that moment, I felt as though I needed to do whatever it took to get to the mountain the next day to teach snowboarding lessons to the little groms.* But with my Explorer broken down on the side of the highway, that was going to be a bit rough. Then the thought came in, "What about my old 1992 Buick LeSabre that had 230,000 miles on it behind the barn chillin'* in the sticker bushes." The car was a gift from my dad, and man that thing had gone the distance, but I thought its days were over. But I went out there and opened the hood, like any man who has no clue about mechanics does, because it makes us feel like we know what's going on. Really all that is happening is we look and see that there is an engine and think, "Yep, looks good to me."

Sure enough, the thing fired up first try. So I packed my stuff in the car that night and finally around 2 am went to bed. Because Crystal Mountain is like 3 hours away, I would have to get up at 5 am. I still wasn't fully convinced this whole thing was actually happening, so I didn't set an alarm (beauty sleep sounded better at the time). The next morning I woke up early, ready to go.

ALL THIS & MORE

I will never forget the sight I saw as I walked outside the door. Everything was completely white, almost a foot of snow had fallen that night. Which was pretty insane, because most winters it doesn't snow much where we live due to the warm air off the Peugeot Sound. I look back on that time now and it makes me think of when God says in Isaiah 1:18, "*Though your sins are like scarlet, they shall be white as snow.*"

I wonder if God was sending me a little hint of what He was about to do.

As I drove through the snow covered roads, I passed 4x4's and SUV's that had spun out of control and got stuck in the storm. But the Buick was a beast. As I got to the base of the mountain, the clouds began to part and the sun began to shine through. As I made it into the parking lot, I realized I had time to take a run before starting work.

It was most definitely the best run of my life, for more reasons than one. Since it was cold enough to snow at the lower elevation, it was extra cold up on the mountain, making for the best snow I had ever been in. In Washington state we usually have what we call "wet cement," which is wet heavy snow, but we would dream about Colorado powder or "champagne powder" (because Colorado gets so cold, the snow is some of the lightest and fluffiest snow in the world.) That day it was like Colorado powder, I know because now I live in Colorado ☺.

I remember stopping in the middle of the woods, covered in snow, with a smile that stretched from ear to ear that could not be wiped away and just yelling at the top of my lungs "SOOOOOOO SIIIIIICCCCCCKKKKKKKKK!" Again, it was like God "spoke" to my heart. He was showing me that He wanted to give me "all this and more." Not money or fame, but He wanted to give me a sense of joy that no one could ever take away. Years later I would read this verse and make the connection, "*No one will take away your joy*" (John 16:22).

I didn't know what it would look like, I didn't know how it was going to end, I didn't even know what it meant. But I knew this was what I wanted. I had been longing for and looking for a joy that wasn't based on a drug, an experience or on what possessions I had, because none of that worked. This was more than a vague feeling, it was a sense of fulfillment that reached into the depths of my soul. I wasn't sure how it would work, but I knew right there and then my life would never be the same.

CHAPTER 10

TAKE A STAND

The next day was Sunday, but rather than going to church with a question for the pastor, I found out he had a question for me.

The pastor gave a sermon that talked about trying to find life, happiness, excitement, satisfaction and joy in all the wrong places. He talked about how true life and joy are only found in a relationship with Jesus—not going to church, not reading the Bible, not saying prayers, but in knowing Jesus. I realized this is what I was missing, I was trying to act the part, but I missed what it was all about. Jesus. The Christian life isn't a bunch of rules or lists of do's and don'ts. Christianity is about a person, Jesus, and a relationship with Him. This resonated in my heart. I knew I couldn't live up to a set of rules, I had enough rules that I already wasn't obeying, last thing I needed was more rules not to follow.

The pastor said, "Stop trying to change yourself, you don't have the power to change on your own. Come as you are, let Jesus change you from the inside out." I realized this is what I needed. This was my only hope. I knew I didn't have the power to change my life on my own. I had tried to quit drugs in the past and I'd ended up in a coma and almost lost my life.

It was the pastor's next words that brought me to my knees and then to my feet, "Jesus lived the life you could never live and then He died the death you deserved to die, paying the penalty you could not pay. And three days later He rose to new life and now is offering His life to you."

This is what is often known as "the great exchange." Jesus took our sin and death and through faith we receive His righteousness and life. Righteousness can be explained as right relationship, referring to the "right relationship" with God that was lost in the Garden when humankind became sinners. But it was earned back by Jesus and freely given to us who believe.

This is salvation. We are saved from the penalty of sin, now and forever. We are saved from the power of sin, giving us the ability to resist temptation (although we don't always live in that reality). When we die, we will experience the saving from the presence of sin as we stand in the presence of our God.

The pastor said, "If you are in here and this is you, then I am going to ask you to do something really bold. I am going to ask you to take a stand." I knew he was talking to me... but there was no way in church I was standing. The dude started praying and the next thing I knew I was standing in the middle of the whole church.

I wish I could tell you that my life was changed right there and then. Like all of a sudden temptation was a thing of the past, that I received powers to walk on water or that my very touch could heal people. But it didn't happen like that. At least not for me. But God began a process in my life. Little by little, starting that day, God began changing my desires and, little by little, no longer would I want to get high or drunk. It's a process that is still going on today. God's not finished, there is a LOT of work still to be done in my life. But it started with me entering into a relationship with Jesus. That is what starts the process.

For me, I physically took a stand, but it was more than a stand. It was a response to God inviting me into a life long relationship with Him. If you're not a Christian, if you have never made a decision to believe in Jesus and live in relationship with Him, then maybe it is your turn to take a stand. Maybe you have been raised in church but you have never made the decision yourself. Going to church doesn't make a person a Christian. Just like going to the mountains of Colorado doesn't make a person a snowboarder. You need a snowboard to be a snowboarder. In the same way, you need Christ to be a Christian.

The sweet thing is you don't have to be led into a prayer by some pastor, nor do you have to go through some crazy

LOVIN' LIFE!

ritual. That is not the stuff that makes a person a Christian. Trusting in Jesus is what makes a person a Christian. And you can do that right now, right where you are at.

I think it is pretty simple. Simple, because Jesus is the one who did all the hard work. Jesus suffered through excruciating torture and died a gruesome death on a Roman cross 2,000 years ago. He died to pay the penalty for our sins. It is through His death and resurrection that we receive new life. Restored relationship with God. This is what we were created for. This is how we experience the fullness of this life. This is worth taking a stand for.

Taking a stand is choosing to say, "I missed the biggest thing in life, a relationship with You, God. I recognize that I have been living for myself and my own selfish desires, rather than living for You. I admit to You that I have done things wrong." The Bible uses the word "repentance," which means to have a change. Mainly referring to the change of mind, changing the way you think about Jesus. Stop un-believing and start believing! Believe that Jesus truly did die on the cross to pay your penalty, believe that Jesus is your hope for life in heaven, but also that He is the key to life now. Believing in this sense is like trusting. In the same way that you trust a chair can hold your weight and so you sit on it, trust Jesus for your salvation.

Then, we say thank you. "Thank You, God. Thank You that You never gave up on me. Thank You for sending Your Son Jesus to die on the cross and pay the penalty for my sin, dying the death I was meant to die. Thank You that You went to such great lengths to show me your love even though I was living for myself. Thank You. I'm trusting in You alone as my strength to live this new life. Thank You." First we say thank you with our lips, then we say thank you with our lives as we continue to strive to become more and more like Jesus through the power He gives through His Spirit that lives in us. Not to earn our salvation, but as a way of thanking God for the gift He has given us.

Romans 10:9 says, "*If you confess with your mouth, 'Jesus is Lord,' and believe in your heart that God raised him from the dead you will be saved.*"

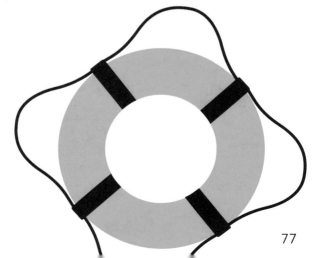

New Life!

Galatians 2:20: "*I have been crucified with Christ and I no longer live, but Christ lives in me. The life I live in the body, I live by faith in the Son of God who loved me and gave himself for me.*"

If you just prayed that prayer, the Bible says that there is a party going on in heaven right now because of you. You've taken a big step, but your adventure is just starting! Don't miss out on all God has waiting for you! Step into this new life as a follower of Jesus with all you've got. Here are a few pieces of advice for you.

Get Planted: You need good soil. If you are not going to a church already, you NEED to start. We were not meant to do this Christian life on our own.

Water the Seed: A sprouting seed needs just the right ingredients in order to thrive. As a new believer, you do too. Things like reading the Bible in order to know God's truth (I'd try 15 minutes per day, starting in

John), talking to God (AKA praying) about anything and everything, journaling (writing down stuff you learn).

Grow: As you grow, you need to GO! God wants you to grow into the Christian He made you to be. He has an amazing life filled with adventure for you that is just now starting. While it's your job to continue to "water the seed," you also need space to stretch your branches. Begin telling other people about the new life you are experiencing with God. Talk to them about stuff you learned in this book and stuff you're learning in the Bible.

Produce Fruit: As you stay planted in good soil and get the water you need to keep growing, you will bear fruit. You will begin to see the fruit of God in your life through your attitude and your actions. Check out Galatians 5:22-23: "*The fruit of the Spirit is love, joy, peace, patience, kindness, goodness, faithfulness, gentleness, and self control.*" You also need to get involved in ministry. Serve at your church. Ask what areas they need help in. As you tell friends about Jesus, invite them along in your life with God. Bring them to church, study the Bible with them and even have times of prayer together.

CHAPTER 11

ALL
IN

There was no looking back. I had begun to experience the greatest joy of my entire life and it didn't come from some drug or from a drunken party. It was the life I had always been looking for. The drugs, parties, drinking and sleeping around with girls had been all about trying to experience the fullness of this life, yet fell short. Like I said, that stuff had been fun, but it hadn't been fulfilling and it had always left me wanting more.

GO BIG or GO HOME

I think I went home after this one.

Like I mentioned earlier, Jesus said to His followers, "*The thief comes only to steal and kill and destroy; I have come that they may have life, and have it to the full*" (John 10:10). Or as The Message version says, "*So they can have real and eternal life, more and better life than they ever dreamed of.*"

That is the life I began to experience in my new relationship with Jesus.

Not a Solo Gig

We were never meant to do the Christian life on our own. When I first became a believer, I instantly started helping out at the church. I'll admit going to a church has often been a little weird for me, because I wasn't use to it. It might be weird for you too, but it is necessary. It can be easy to go to church and be critical about the things you don't like—boring, long, doesn't make sense or whatever. But church wasn't meant to be a bystander sport, we are meant to get involved. It's difficult to be bored or critical if you are a part of it.

You could volunteer in the youth group or children's ministry. Or if you have musical talents, offer to help out with the praise band. Maybe you want to be more in the background. You could help out with setup, clean up or even with the sound and video department. There could even be opportunities through other ministries that your church has. Ask around, pray about it, and get plugged in.

Within two months of my making the decision to believe in Jesus, I ended up helping with the youth group and meeting a girl. It wasn't like that...well okay, maybe I was crushing a little bit. But she ended up moving to New Zealand to go to a Torchbearer Bible School. We kept in contact just long enough for her to tell me that there was another school just like the one she was going to, but it was in the mountains of Colorado, right next to a ski resort. I was still pretty new to this whole Jesus thing, so the idea of Bible School kinda freaked me out, but the idea of living next to a ski resort got me thinking.

That night I checked out the Torchbearer website and found out they had schools all over the world! They even had one on a sailboat in Greece! Greece sounded sick,* but Colorado had me at hello. It turns out there are two schools in Colorado. I didn't know how to decide between the two, so I did the whole eney meeny miny moe and landed on Timberline Lodge in Winter Park, Colorado. I called the next day to find out about school, only to learn that it started in two weeks. I told them I was coming. They tried telling me I had to register, get accepted and pay tuition first; but I didn't let any of that hoopla distract me, I was ready to snowboard!

I put my two week notice resignation in at the beer company that night, even though I hadn't even been accepted into the school yet. I wish you could have seen the look on the dudes' faces I worked with when I told them I was going to Bible School! These were dudes I had partied hard with and now as far as they were concerned, I was going to be a priest.

I got accepted a couple days later, but still didn't have enough money for tuition. I was trying to sell my four cars to help foot the bill, but then I wouldn't have a way to get there. Four days before school started, I ended up selling the car I had bought with drug money, cash for the amount I was asking. And then a couple families I

Life is AWESOME at Timberline!

knew, who knew about the old life I'd lived, were willing to do just about anything to help since I wasn't making stupid decisions anymore (or at least not as stupid of decisions).

Three days before I was supposed to leave, I was pricing out airline tickets, when my dad called, asking if I was still thinking about this Bible School thing (he thought I was a bit crazy). I told him I was going, I just wasn't sure how to get there. My dad ended up taking care of my airline ticket with air miles he had earned from all his business travel.

Looking back, I see the fingerprint of God, He was the one who truly hooked me up. God used the Torchbearer School to change my life forever. It wasn't so much the classes that did it for me, it was the friends and the time I got to spend just me and Jesus. Every day I would go outside and spend time reading my Bible and just talking to God. My original intention with going to

Bible School was to live in Colorado and shred at least 100 days that winter.

God changed all that when I got there. When I lived in Washington, I would snowboard 50-60 days a year, and I lived two hours from the mountain. Living in Colorado, I could snowboard in my backyard, but I only went riding 20 days that year. It was like I found something so much more rewarding, satisfying and fulfilling. Jesus says, "*Blessed are those who hunger and thirst for righteousness,*" righteousness is like a right relationship with God, "*for they shall be satisfied*" (Matthew 5:6).

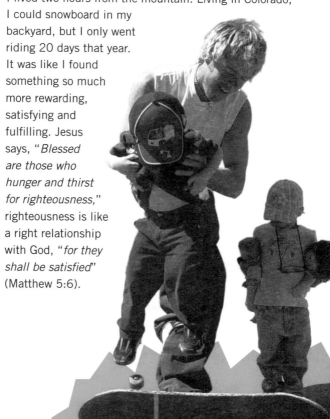

It wasn't like I was forcing myself not to snowboard, locking myself in my room, forcing myself to like God, as if God wants to take away the things we enjoy. It was like, the more time I spent getting to know God, through reading the Bible and praying, the more I desired to know Him better. Not as some sort of duty, but because I was finding joy, purpose and fulfillment in knowing Him in new ways. Then it was like I would have to force myself to go snowboard! People can tell us that a relationship with God is awesome, but hearing about that relationship isn't anywhere near as exciting as experiencing it for ourselves.

It's kinda like if you never snowboarded in your entire life, and one day we are hanging out and I tell you about how legit* snowboarding is. Let's say as you hear how stoked I am on snowboarding, you decide you believe me. You still haven't experienced just how rad snowboarding is yet. So you look up some YouTube videos and you are amazed. But you still don't know it for yourself. So then you get online and purchase a full set up: board, boots, goggles, hat, jacket, pants, gloves and even hand warmers (which is weird because you live in Hawaii—remember it's make believe, and Hawaii is where I would want to live in make believe land). You still haven't experienced snowboarding.

So finally you get a plane ticket to visit me in Coloradical. We go to the top of the mountain, because you are feeling dangerous, you strap in and push off. You can feel the wind begin to rush against your face, you hear

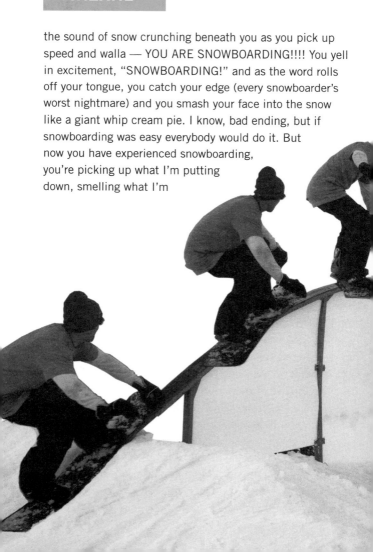

the sound of snow crunching beneath you as you pick up speed and walla — YOU ARE SNOWBOARDING!!!! You yell in excitement, "SNOWBOARDING!" and as the word rolls off your tongue, you catch your edge (every snowboarder's worst nightmare) and you smash your face into the snow like a giant whip cream pie. I know, bad ending, but if snowboarding was easy everybody would do it. But now you have experienced snowboarding, you're picking up what I'm putting down, smelling what I'm stepping in, you know what I am talking about when I say it's sick.

I could tell you until I am blue in the face that snowboarding is one of the sickest experiences in the world and you might believe me. It doesn't matter how convincing I may be, you still can't truly know it for yourself until you experience it. Same is true with Jesus. You may have all the right gear, Bible, cross necklace and even go to church,

RAD!

but that doesn't mean you have experienced Christ and the fullness He has to offer. In order to experience the fullness that Christ has for you, it takes going "ALL IN."

For me, I had to leave some things behind. I had to stop doing some of the things I was doing in order to experience what Jesus had in store. For me, that actually meant leaving my home, friends and old way of life. In doing that, I experienced a whole new way of life. Jesus wants you to experience the fullness of this life, too. (Remember, John 10:10 about Jesus promising real, abundant and full life.) But so many Christians miss experiencing all that Jesus has for them. Often the reason they miss it is because there are things getting in the way, they aren't willing to leave the old way of life. It's hard to experience the fullness of snowboarding when you're still sitting on the couch watching videos about it.

So many people ride the fence with one foot in the church and the other foot in the world. They believe in Jesus and sing the songs at church, but it doesn't affect the way they live their lives outside the walls of the church. It can be easy to act one way around other Christians and then be a totally different person everywhere else. For them, Christianity becomes more about how good a person can act, rather than experiencing the very purpose for which they were made.

No wonder so many people think Christianity is boring; I would too if it was just about going to church, not swearing and acting right. God desires more from us and for us than just our Sunday's. He wants our entire lives. We will never be fully content and fulfilled until we are ready to go "ALL IN" and live for Him.

Maybe you have been a Christian for a long time, but you have never experienced the excitement, joy and fullness that I am talking about. Have you tried? What if you were to take God at His word and believe that true, real and abundant joy was found in getting to know Jesus better? What if you decided to spend time with Jesus rather than filling your time with video games, movies, sports and social media? What if you start to find time to read your Bible, pray, hang out with other believers, serve at your church, go on a missions trip or even start telling friends about Jesus?

What if you decided to go "ALL IN" for Jesus?

Experiencing God's Love to the Fullest

"Early one morning I was tackled by Zane's enthusiasm
for the Word of God. What surprised me was which
verse had ignited his intense excitement. By the look of
his big smile, I thought he had unlocked a real treasure.
I thought it might have been a misplaced verse in the
Old Testament that I had overlooked in my 20+ years of
growing up in the church. I was ready for Zane to amaze
me and then he shared this verse: *"For God so loved the
world that He gave His only Son!"*

"John 3:16...really?" I cynically thought to myself. I
never realized someone could have grown up without
ever digesting that verse. How did Zane miss it? But
more than that, how did Zane get so excited about John
3:16? As he read the verse to me, he crescendoed into
the last word, almost shouting and spitting joy into my
face. I had no response early that morning other than to
affirm that it certainly was a good verse.

You see, Zane literally ate up the Bible during those
first years of Bible School, like he had been starved for
the last 20 years, deprived of what he really needed. He
was satisfied by the simple truth that God loved him.
I think I often look for God to amaze me by something

new or edgy or relevant, based on how good the teacher or preacher is at church.

But Zane was amazed by the simple message of God's love as he read his Bible, because it changed him so radically from the inside out. I saw joy on his face, not because of the words he read, but because of what the words meant to him. Zane LOVED Jesus and on that morning it was as if he realized how much God LOVED Zane.

Zane reminded me that morning how exciting it is to be rooted in the Word of God. Psalm 1 describes how the godly person finds his or her delight in God's Word every day, meditating on it day and night. What things do you think about all the time? If you are like me, I typically meditate about the things I care most about in my life. Do you believe God's Word is capable of your constant attention?

The Bible promises that the Spirit will illuminate our hearts with the deep and profound truths of God. I witnessed that promise in Zane that morning and have since realized I have full access to the same excitement Zane showed me for God's Word because of the Spirit of God inside of me."

—Phil Peterson

CHAPTER 12
BROS, PROS AND' GROMS

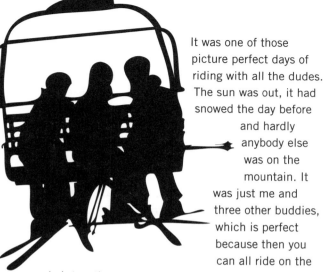

It was one of those picture perfect days of riding with all the dudes. The sun was out, it had snowed the day before and hardly anybody else was on the mountain. It was just me and three other buddies, which is perfect because then you can all ride on the same chair together, no one gets left behind and no weird people get on the lift with you.

As we were approaching the lift, my buddy Wilson got this wild look on his face and broke away from our group, barely dodging the chair that was coming around to load the two people in front of us. He jumped on their chairlift. Then he looked back at us, giving the thumbs up.

We quickly realized that the lift he had gotten on had two girls on it. So we all started cracking up, yelling, whistling and talking trash. There was no one else in line and Wilson had made a mad dash for the chair with the girls on it.

INZANE

So we got on the next chair still somewhat amazed that
our buddy just ditched us to ride up with some cute girls
on the chair in front of us. But we didn't let it faze us and
within seconds we were back to guy talk. You know, poop,
farts and all sorts of other real important topics.

About halfway up the chair ride it hit me, "I bet Wilson is
telling those girls about Jesus." You see Wilson was one of
the students I got to spend a lot of time with over his year
at the Torchbearer School. We would often talk about going
all in for Jesus and not being afraid to talk about Him with
other people. I had a feeling in my gut that Wilson was
living it out right then and there.

ME AND A FEW OF MY
BROS AT TIMBERLINE

So I interrupted the in depth guy talk on the lift, "Hey guys, I bet Wilson is telling those girls about Jesus." Silence fell on the group. We all knew it was true, because that is the type of guy Wilson is.

Marshall then piped up, "Here we are talking about poop and Wilson is telling people about Jesus. Maybe we should pray instead. You know, pray that God would use Wilson to speak to those girls."

It was awesome, we went from talking about poop to partnering with our friend through prayer as he shared the amazing message of Jesus with two random strangers.

Sure enough, when we got off the chair and asked Wilson how the chair ride was, he had a story about his amazing conversation with the two girls about Jesus.

That changed our entire day of riding, because every time we would get in line for the lift, Wilson would slide ahead and join a different group. Then he would look back, taunting us to join the challenge to step outside of our comfort zone and embark on this crazy adventure, as well.

It was an epic day!!!! I mean, we still teased Wilson like any good friend would. You know, jokes about "flirt to convert," "missionary dating" and anything else we could think of to not let him off the hook.

But something important happened that day—we four Christian friends prodded each other to "go all in for Jesus."

And our experience on the mountain was a real world example of why you need other Christian friends in your life.

You see, at the Bible School I have made lifelong friends. And I discovered how impacting these friends are in my life with God. I learned that I need to have three sets of people in my life to help me with my walk with God. I need a Bro, someone who is around my age with a similar passion for God that I can kick it with. Someone who also loves Jesus and is trying to figure out what it is to live for Him, so we can encourage each other along the way. But I also need a

GOD REALLY KNOWS HOW TO LAY IT OU

Pro, someone who is older and more mature than me who has been walking with God for longer than me, to give advice and keep me on track. Lastly, I need a Grom, someone who is younger or not as far along in their relationship with God. It is often the Groms who I learn the most from, as I have the opportunity to give back what has been given to me.

It has been the same for me as I tried to get better at snowboarding. I loved having dudes I could ride with who were at my same ability. These were the dudes I rode with every day and we would push each other to get better, my Bros. But if you really want to advance, it helps to know some real rippers.* You know, guys who are so far ahead that it gives you something to aim for, the Pros. But you also gotta share the love and help out the young bucks, the Groms. It is sometimes the Groms who come up with new creative ways to do stuff that inspire the rest of us.

That is what happened at the Bible School. And I still have people in each of these groups in my life—Bros, Pros and Groms. All of them keep encouraging me to go bigger, to not play it safe and to go all in for Jesus. I think you need the same.

Looking for ideas on how you can build this kind of team in your own life? Here are a few tips:

1. Be patient, these types of friendships don't happen overnight.
2. Look around you, maybe these people are already in your life, you just need to be more intentional about those relationships.
3. The Pro – Ask your youth pastor if he or she knows someone who could be a mentor for you.
4. The Bro – Many of us already have these, but maybe we just need to talk with them and see if they want to help us grow in our relationship with God. Maybe start memorizing Scripture together. Maybe you challenge each other to read the Bible. Maybe it's that together you join a Bible study, or start one yourself.
5. The Grom – Church can be a great place to find kids in this group. See about helping out in the children's ministry. Or maybe be intentional about becoming friends with one of the younger kids in youth group. Ask them about their relationship with God. Every once in

a while, share with them what you are learning about God.

Again, a youth pastor can be a great resource to ask as you try to find your Bros, Pros and Groms. And you don't have to just sit around, read the Bible and pray. Do fun stuff together and talk about God as you do it, like me and my buddies snowboarding. Remember, Jesus said He came to give us life to the full! So go camping and bring a guitar for a little worship time. Or next time you're hanging out playing sports, video games or whatevs, just put on some music by Christian artists.

Party at the "Black Shack."

THAT'S WHAT THE STUDENTS CALL OUR HOUSE.

INZANE

Some of my buddies and I started working out and we would put on a sermon while we were pumping iron. You can download free podcasts through iTunes, one of my favorites is by one of my mentors, one of the Pros in my life, Derwin Gray former NFL football player turned pastor who preaches at Transformation Church. Download ALL of his podcasts, and prepare to have your world rocked.

CHAPTER 13
SAME OLD
ZANE

Since that first year at Bible School, I feel like I have been on the craziest adventure in my entire life. I've seen God do exceedingly and abundantly above all that I could ever ask or imagine and it hasn't been because of some special talent I have, but according to God's power within me (Ephesians 3:20).

After spending nine months at the Bible School they asked if I would accept a staff position as assistant program coordinator. Which basically meant that I got to take students and guest youth groups mountain biking, hiking, river rafting, climbing, tubing, snowboarding and all sorts of other ill* stuff. Let's just say I have loved my job, especially because my friend, Phil, was the program coordinator and he did all the real work while I pretty much got to play. So people ended up calling me the "Director of Careless Activities," which I thought suited me a lot better, too. I also had the opportunity to share my story and God's work in my life with the youth groups that would come to Timberline Lodge for ski trips and summer camps.

The crazy thing was that as I would share about my story, students would actually listen! Which is pretty amazing, because later friends would tell me how horrible I actually was at public speaking, but they just didn't have the heart to tell me at the time. Still for some reason, these youth groups began to invite me to visit their hometowns to speak for different youth events. I would get invited to speak at other summer camps, winter camps and even Sunday services! I loved it and still do! It's like I get to hang out with friends all day doing sweet stuff and then talk about what's most important to me, Jesus.

Then one day God dropped a whole new, fun, on-the-edge kind of opportunity to talk to people about Jesus on my plate. This crazy guy, Greg Stier, who is the president of an organization called Dare 2 Share (D2S) was going to film a reality series called *GOSPEL Journey*® at Timberline Lodge. This DVD series was designed to train students on how to talk about God with all different kinds of people. The plan was to take students from lots of different religions and worldviews, go on some super sweet adventures and tell them about Jesus.

Since I worked at Timberline Lodge, I was going to help by showing them the best places to film and by taking them on the different adventures. Well, two days before the film crew came for the shoot they asked if I would be willing to be a part of "the cast" and be "The Guide." I was stoked, even though I had no idea what that meant.

I will never forget the time I got to spend with the *Gospel Journey* crew in the mountains of Colorado for that week. It turned out to be far more than just a "reality series" that discussed the existence of God. It was a week that changed my life. During that week we built some amazing friendships as we talked about the things that meant the most to us. We had different beliefs, awkward moments and disagreements, but through it all, we became great friends. I learned that when you are willing to take risks and talk about Jesus, there is the chance you can get shut down, but it also gives opportunity for interactions that change lives. The conversations, friendships and experiences of that week have been forever imprinted into my mind.

The filming of GOSPEL Journey was an experience like I never had before.

Since *Gospel Journey*, I have gotten to travel with the D2S conference tour as one of their event speakers, talking to thousands of teenagers each year all across the country. And I've gotten to be a part of a second reality series D2S filmed called *Gospel Journey Maui*. I coauthored a book with that crazy man, Greg Stier, called *Shreddin the Gnar* and I wrote this book you're reading right now (just in case you forgot)!

It blows me away to look back at all God has done in and through me. Not only do I feel like God has used me in some awesome ways to tell others about this abundant life available with this amazing Jesus dude, but He has also used me to help others realize that in God's eyes there's no such thing as a lost cause. If God can give me the strength to overcome drugs, getting drunk, sleeping around and all sorts of other poor habits that I had developed, then it's as clear as a crystal blue ocean that He can draw anyone back into a restored relationship with Him. If God didn't see me as a lost cause, then no one is.

What could be better than snorkeling in Maui? | Being with the cast of GOSPEL Journey Maui!

I really have been blessed to experience God use me through these amazing opportunities, but because I strive to be 100% honest in all I say and do, I have to tell you the whole truth. It hasn't been all easy. Even though God has used me and given me great victories, there have been times when I don't live it. There have been times when I fail, times when I fall and I doubt. And I wonder, what if God gives up on me?

One of the biggest areas of struggle for me is lust. It had been a part of my life since puberty, but before I was a Christian I never saw it as a problem. But after I'd been a Christian awhile, I realized this was a battle I wasn't winning. I thought if I put the right things in place, I could have victory over this too. After all, I have been sober for 10 years now and if I wanted God to keep using me, I would have get victory over lust as well.

But this struggle has not gone away. I would tell myself that if I couldn't get victory in this area, then God would stop blessing me with the opportunities to preach His message.

It turns out I'm just not that strong.

So I would begin to feel like God was going to give up on me. I mean, I know that God has forgiven me of my past, but what about when I continue to do the things He hates. Is there a point where God says, "I have forgiven you over

109

and over and now I am done with you?" I now know I am not the only one that feels this way. I have had tons of students come up to me with tears in their eyes, telling me how much they have failed (not just in areas like lust, but getting drunk, anger, unforgiveness, self harm, etc.) and asking if it's too late. Feeling like they couldn't go to God anymore after letting Him down so much.

If you have ever felt like I have, I want to tell you something that changed my life and could change yours. If you believe in Jesus to forgive you of your sin, you trust in Him and Him alone to save you...then you are FORGIVEN. The fact that you feel bad for the areas where you have failed is often a sign that the Spirit of God is alive and at work in your soul.

If you think you have done something "too bad" or "too often" to be forgiven, then it is like you are saying that you know better than God and in a sense you are putting yourself in His position by declaring what can and can't be forgiven. God the Father sent His one and only Son Jesus to die in order to pay the penalty of ALL our sin. Past. Present. Future. All our SIN. Jesus' last words were "it is finished." If you believe in Jesus, then your penalty has been paid in full.

This is GRACE!!!!! It is a gift that you and I do not deserve, it's a gift. We actually can't earn it; we can only receive it through faith (believing, trusting). Once we fully understand this gift, it makes us want to live a life that is pleasing to God. Not because we have to, or in order to earn something, but because we have already received the greatest gift in the world and it's our way of saying thanks.

It's kinda like this, (go to make believe land again), pretend that I came up to you and offered you the gift of "ONE MILLION DOLLARS." What would you do? Hopefully, you would accept my gift. Then let's say I asked you to take me out to lunch, would you do it? Or would you kick dirt on me, spit on me and walk away? NO. I hope you would take me straight to the Golden Arches, order me a "Happy Meal" and that you would even super size it, if that's possible, because I want the toy, but I also love those gloriously greasy fries. I hope our friendship wouldn't end

SPEAKING AT
CREATION
FEST

there. I would hope that you would want to call me every once in a while, maybe go hang out and hopefully you would even tell people about the nice thing I did for you. Not to earn the million dollars, but because you were so thankful for the gift.

That is the same thing with the gift of life we receive from Jesus, it's a gift. Romans 6:23 says, "*The wages of sin is death, but the FREE gift of God is eternal life in Christ Jesus our Lord*" (ESV). We didn't do anything to earn it or deserve it. "*But God demonstrates his own love for us in this: While we were still sinners, Christ died for us*" (Romans 5:8). The gift of life was very costly, it cost Jesus everything and us nothing. You didn't do anything to earn your salvation, nor can you do anything to un-earn your salvation.

{ **Hangin' at a speaking event**
with two of my mentors (Pros) – Rolly (a wise sage and also event producer) and Greg (preacher extraordinaire and also Dare 2 Share prez).

Looking back, I realized all the conferences, camps, reality series, books and other ways God has used me haven't been because of me in the first place. It was all because of God's grace, He chose to use me and it wasn't anything that I had in and of myself. If it depended on me, who knows where I'd be? I know one thing, it wouldn't be worth writing a book about. That is what gives me the desire and drive to keep fighting for victory in the battle against sin. It's my way of saying thank you to God.

Is your life lived as one big THANK YOU to God?

Or

Did you say thank you once and now you're living for your own desires and passions?

I believe God has a great plan for your life and the possibilities are limitless.

These areas of sin can get in the way and take our focus off Jesus, causing us to miss some of the amazing things He has for us.

God has plans to do *"exceedingly and abundantly more than all we ask or imagine, according to His power that is at work within us"* (Ephesians 3:20).

I could have never accomplished all that has happened since becoming a Christian in my own strength, but that is the beauty of the Christian life. Not only did Jesus die to pay the penalty for our sin, but He also rose to new life and offers His life to us! Moment by moment every day we have the opportunity to live beyond our own capabilities, empowered by the strength of Jesus who lives in us. One of the writers in the Bible says this is the mystery that people throughout all history have been waiting for: *"Christ in you, the hope of glory"* (Colossians 1:27). When you become a Christian, no longer do you have to live according to your own strength, but the fullness of God is fully available to you (Colossians 1:19, Galatians 2:20).

I wish we all grasped the fullness of that reality. I wish I grasped the fullness of that reality. Imagine how our lives would be different.

May we strive for victory in our war against sin, but not according to our own strength, but according to God's strength through us.

Looking for ideas on how to wrestle against sin? Try wrestling WWF Style.

I use to watch WWF as a kid. I would get so mad when my dad would tell me it was fake. It couldn't be fake; I was watching it right before my very eyes! Turns out he was right. I guess they have it all planned out who wins. Well guess what, in our struggle against sin, one day we will win for good. We know how it ends; when this life is over we will be in the presence of Jesus, with victory over every area of sin. So remember WWF. It goes like this:

WORD Memorization: Commit God's Word to memory and you will have a sword to fight with. Scripture tells us that the Word of God is like a double-edged sword to do battle with, waging war against our sin. And Psalm 119:11 says, *"I have hidden your word in my heart that I might not sin against you."*

Worship: Spend your energy on making much of Jesus. Don't spend all your thoughts and energy on how to battle your sin, focus your energy on finding satisfaction, joy and fulfillment in Jesus. As you begin to find your all in Jesus, your desire for these lesser things will begin to fall away. Focus on Him, not the sin. Maybe even download some worship music on your iPod and listen to it more often. Play it in your room, when you workout or in your car. I personally like David Crowder.

Friends: Get other guys (or if you are a girl, other girls) to check in on you, to ask how you are doing. But not just on whether or not you have failed, but to check on how you are doing in your relationship with God. Sin is usually a lack of understanding of what we have in Christ. Meet regularly with these friends, encourage one another often. Hebrews 3:13 says *"encourage one another each day...If you don't, then sin may fool some of you and make you stubborn"* (CEV).

But if you forget about the WWF, just remember Jesus. He is what's most important. Last I checked, it's all about Him. If you are a believer, Jesus lives in you through the power of His Spirit. Ask Him to give you the strength and focus on His power.

CHAPTER 14
LIT

I remember going back home to visit friends and family in Seattle and getting invited to a party with all my old friends. So I went. I felt a bit awkward at first, as people were getting drunk and high. A group of us were standing in a circle and as usual everybody was trying to impress each other with stories of the last party, or the one time when they got super hammered and did something stupid. Which is funny to me, that these are the things that often get bragged about. In the middle of all the hot air, someone busted out a pipe and began to pass it around.

Like it or not, I found myself in the midst of the smoke out circle, and before I had time to think, the pipe got passed to me. It was as if time stood still. I hadn't seen most of these guys for over a year and they had no clue about me becoming a Christian. What should I do? If I just passed it on, people were going to think I was a freak for not hittin' it. Then I realized everybody was waiting for me, apparently I had thought about it for too long, because the conversation stopped. I guess time did not stand still; the clock was ticking all along. All eyes were on me.

I don't know what I was thinking, but I went for it, I couldn't help it. I just started talking about Jesus, pipe still in hand and all. People definitely did not expect that, but they sure were a captive audience. So I shared the gospel the best I knew how and people listened. Well, they sort of listened, about as good as a bunch of half-baked stoners could. Some were probably just spacing out, having no clue what I was talking about, but I know that at least a couple dudes heard what I was saying. Because when I got done, the dude next to me was like, "Jesus is *&%-ing rad man."

I probably would have used a different descriptive word than the dude did, but I think Jesus is pretty rad, too. Looking back, I also would not recommend putting yourself in a compromising situation like I did. That probably wasn't the smartest thing I have done and there are a lot better ways to reach our friends than by holding the "peace pipe," talking about Jesus when everybody else is in a state of comatose thinking about munchies.

One thing hasn't changed since then. Regardless of where I am, I can't not talk about Jesus. It's just that the more stoked I've gotten on Jesus, the more I talk about Him. I know that some people feel it is not socially acceptable to talk about spiritual things because it is a private matter. I know that people don't want it shoved down their throats. I know that people disagree and even sometimes get mad when others talk about Jesus. But here is the deal, I CAN'T STOP!

When I first came to Bible School, one of the guys took me out street witnessing (telling strangers about Jesus on the streets). I was so new to Christianity, that I didn't know what was socially acceptable, nor did I have a smooth way of bringing God up in conversation. So I would just ask, straight up, "Do you know Jesus?" People would respond with things like, "I believe in evolution, or I was raised Baptist, or I go to a Catholic church." I would be like, "Sweet, so what do you think about Jesus?" To me, I didn't care whether a person grew up Baptist, went to a Catholic church, or even if they believed in evolution. I wanted to know if they loved Jesus.

For me, that is all that mattered – JESUS.

It was Jesus that I was excited about. Experiencing life with Jesus is not about what church we grew up in, what group we belong to or the things we believe about science. The way to experience life with Jesus is by getting to know Him. So I wanted to know if people knew Jesus. So when people would try to argue with me about whatever, I would just talk about Jesus, because I was stoked on Jesus. Everybody thought I was crazy!

It's true, I was crazy about Jesus, so I couldn't hold it back. Over the years, I have learned more about how to bring

Jesus up in normal conversation. As that has happened, I have still had some people tell me that I need to chill out and not talk about Jesus so much because it offends people. I've tried doing what they say. It doesn't work. I feel like the prophet Jeremiah when he said, "*If I say, 'I will not mention Him or speak any more in His name,' his word is in my heart like a fire, a fire shut up in my bones. I am weary of holding it in; indeed, I cannot*" (Jeremiah 20:9).

I think we talk about the things we love. Hang out with any group of people for long enough and you will know about the things they like and dislike. Every time I talk to my friends that still get high, they tell me about the last time they were super messed up or the girl they just hooked up with. So I think that gives us permission to do the same, we can talk about what's most important to us, Jesus. I would assume that your friends aren't trying to force you to get high with them (if they are, they are not real friends and you should ditch them). Nor should we try and force our friends to become Christians. But we should let them know about how much we are stoked on Jesus and we should have convincing proof that Jesus is worth being stoked on.

So our job is to get stoked on Jesus. When this happens, it will naturally flow out of your life. You won't be able to hold it back.

What if you have been holding it back?

Maybe then it's time to get a little crazy for Jesus?

Begin to pray every morning a quick prayer right before you get out of bed. Try this: "God, get me stoked on You today, and allow this stoke to overflow to the lives of my friends."

ME & THE WIFE
DRESSING UP FOR
STAFF PHOTOS

Think of one friend who doesn't know Jesus. Start praying for this friend, asking God to draw them closer to Himself. Pray right now. This week tell someone at church about how you want your stoke to overflow into the lives of your non-believing friends. Ask if they would pray for your stoke not to die down, to pray for a heart change for your unbelieving friend.

Even the apostle Paul asked other people to pray for him in this way in Ephesians 6:19-20, "*Pray also for me, that whenever I open my mouth, words may be given me so that I will fearlessly make known the mystery of the gospel... Pray that I may declare it fearlessly, as I should.*"

Lit
What gets you lit?

The Spark: Is hell your motivation, or is it because God says, or heaven? The thing that gets me motivated is that I just don't want people to miss out on the life that Jesus wants to give them today. So when I share, I talk a lot about how sweet life is with Jesus now.

"Stoke" the Fire: The more wood, the more fire. Get other friends to join you in reaching your other friends with the gospel. You will burn brighter together. So get stoked. In the same way dudes get pumped up for the big game by listening to pump up music, I have a list of bands that I rock out with to get me stoked, stoked on Jesus. I like hip hop, so I listen to guys like Lecrae and Propaganda.

Fan the Flame: Pray, asking God for the power of His Spirit to go beyond your own abilities. How cool is it that it's not really dependent upon us, but on God? Pray daily, asking God to keep the fire going. Ask Him to show you the people to share with and ask Him to change the hearts of those who don't know Him.

CHAPTER 15
THE
CAUSE

Okay, so now you're all stoked on Jesus and ready to share that stoke with the world, but how do you do it?

Growing up outside of Seattle on this little island called Camano Island, I lived two hours away from some of the sickest snowboarding in the U.S., a place called Mt. Baker. Baker is legendary for having some of the most epic dumps (not like the kind you leave in the porcelain pool), but the white snow kind. Baker is actually an active volcano and because of its location, it gets hammered with snow. In March of 2011, it got six feet in five days and in the 1998-99 ski season, Baker set the world record for snowfall with 1,140 inches of snow, which is almost 100 feet of snow!!!!

With all that snow, it produced perfect conditions for dropping cliffs. The sweet thing was, it didn't even matter if you landed straight on your head, which was good for me. Some dudes have hucked* some pretty big cliffs, one of the biggest cliffs dropped was by a dude named Jamie Pierre who launched a cliff that was 256 feet. Unfortunately he did land on his head, but fortunately he was okay.

So I was out riding with my buddies one day after a huge dump and we were on a cliff dropping mission. I spotted a cliff from the chairlift that looked pretty dece,* but it was far from the 256' mark, more along the 26' mark. We rode through the woods trying to find it, but ended up coming to a big roped off area that had caution tape to keep people out, I think it said something like "Do not cross, will die" or something. Now my disclaimer is that this was before I was a Christian. So I ducked the rope and kept riding. All my buddies were like, "What are you doin' man, that thing is there for a reason."

I was like, "Yeah, to keep people like you from having fun, I'm going for it." Next thing I knew, I was all alone in the woods, looking for this cliff that I wanted to huck my carcass off. Sure enough, I came up to this pretty big drop off and it looked like the same cliff I spotted from the chairlift. Since I was not sure, I started getting a little scared because I couldn't fully see if it was a legit drop off, or if it had jagged rocks sticking out. As I slid closer to the edge, eventually I came to the point of no return. Either I took my board off and hiked out or I gave 'er all I got so I'd have enough speed to clear the protruding rocks.

Pep talk. I started convincing myself in my head that I had to go for it. I have always been the type of person to go all out in life, like I said earlier, we got one life and I wanted to make the most of it. I didn't think it all the way through and consider that going for it could mean losing that one life. Regardless, I let out this yell like I was some warrior ready to charge the enemy screaming freedom with my face painted all blue. Then I went for it.

As I made the turn to point toward the edge of the cliff, I caused an avalanche. The whole area on which I was standing broke and it began taking me off the cliff. Except

it was taking me off the cliff upside down, my face was now looking at the cliff and my head was flying by those rock that I was hoping to miss. This was not how I'd envisioned it going during my pep talk. I ended up landing on my back with my legs above me at the bottom of the cliff and all the snow from the avalanche landed on top of me and I was completely buried.

I'd heard that you have an average of 7-14 minutes to survive if you are buried in an avalanche. So I tried not to panic and I started thinking as quickly as I could. The first thing that came to my mind was "I need air." Brilliant I know, but true. I noticed that I could move one hand, so I began trying to wiggle it free. Then I started digging as best as I could with that one hand. It was like finding gold when I felt the surface of the snow with the tips of my finger. I immediately started digging out my face as quickly as I could. It was like I had been held underwater till about the point of drowning. I came out of that snow like a sea monkey rising from the deep, gasping for air with an inhale that could have sucked the

I'LL SAVE YOU ZANE!

pine needles off the trees had they been close enough. I unburied myself and practically crawled over to the nearest tree and when I got to it, I just hugged it. Gave it a big ole warm embrace, held it tight telling it how happy I was to see it again. I guess after all, I am a tree hugger.

As I was having this intimate moment...with a tree, I looked across the valley and spotted a dude stuck in the same position I'd been. Buried at the bottom of a cliff, but this guy's feet were sticking out. So I did what any guy would do. I laughed, poor sucker. Then I realized the dude couldn't get out. His legs were kicking and I realized I had to do something. So I started riding across the valley, weaving in and out of trees. As I got closer, the guy's legs started slowing down. People had spotted the guy from down below (because he did not cross the "do not cross will die" rope but stuck close to the chairlift), and people had taken off their skis and boards and they were running up the hill to rescue this guy.

Before anyone got there, his legs stopped moving. The people from below got to him before I did and they started unburying him. As they got him unburied, they pulled him out of the hole. His body looked lifeless. They ripped off his jacket and immediately started CPR. One person was holding the head, another person was doing chest compressions and yelling 1, 2, 3,...and then all of a sudden, the dude was like the sea monkey I mentioned before, coming out of the deep, gasping for air like he was trying to suck the needles off the surrounding trees. I was like, "Yep, air, that's good stuff, huh man."

I feel like in a lot of ways that story sums up my life. I feel like for 21 years of my life it was like I was buried, suffocating, separated from the very thing I needed to live and my time was running out. Becoming a Christian was like coming out of the avalanche when my face first saw the daylight as the last handful of snow was removed and I could take in that breathe of fresh air.

When I became a Christian it was like God gave me a new breath to breathe, a new life to live, He rescued me from being separated not from air, but from Him, true

ME AND MY BRIDE!

Livin' THE Cause together

life. But it didn't stop there. I had an intimate moment with a tree (no spiritual application there) and then it was like I was sent on a mission to help other people who have been stuck, suffocating, buried under the weight of sin, gasping for life. I've been sent on a mission to do whatever it takes to help people just like me find true, real and abundant life, just like I did.

This is your mission, too. At Dare 2 Share, we call it "THE Cause." There are so many causes in the world. Save this butterfly, hug that tree, but the greatest cause of all is THE Cause of Jesus. Jesus was on a mission to make disciples who make disciples and now this is our mission. Jesus said in John 20:21, "*As the father sent me, I am sending you.*" This is THE Cause.

It is best summed up in a great passage known as "The Great Commission." Well, I never really knew what "Commission" meant. Which is also why I just like calling it THE Cause. In Matthew 28:18-20, Jesus gives sort of a last challenge, a final send off to His friends, telling them that He is ruler over all the heavens and earth. With that understanding as the foundation, Jesus wants them to go all over the world and show people what it looks like to be stoked on Him. He tells them to baptize new believers in the name of the Father, Son and Holy Spirit, and to teach these new believers what it really looks like to follow God and how to get others to follow God. And then Jesus promises them that although this is a big task, His presence will always be with them, for He will live inside of them through His Spirit. Now that is pretty cool stuff, THE Cause.

GET THE WORD OUT!

So I would like to invite you, will you live THE Cause, too?

Start by PRAYING. Pray for your friends who don't know Jesus, that they'd get to know Him. Pray for your friends who are Christians, that they would join you and Jesus in this thing called THE Cause. If you don't know any non-Christians, then pray and ask God to put people in your life who don't know Jesus.

Follow up by PURSUING. Look for opportunities to tell your non-Christian friends about how stoked you are on Jesus. Give them this book if you want, or if this is too heavy duty, give them the little booklet *Get Stoked* that's specifically written for you to share with your unreached friends. (You'll find a sample copy of *Get Stoked* printed into the back of this book, so you can look it over before you pick some up for your friends.) Tell them if they don't like it, they can use it as toilet paper. Whether they like it or not, you can use it to get the conversation about Jesus out on the table. But whether you use *InZane, Get Stoked*, or something else, at least try to bring Jesus up with one person today. You can try by mentioning something that gets you fired up about Jesus. Start making this a habit, with the goal of doing it once a day. Just slip it into casual conversation. Or even ask one of your friends what they believe. Let them talk, you listen, and then you can even ask more questions.

Get Stoked

Get Stoked is a short little comic booklet type deal I wrote to help you get a Jesus conversation going with your friends. It's a shortened version of my story plus the amazing message of Jesus' love and forgiveness. Check out the sample in the back of this book and then pick up some full-color versions for your friends. You can get them at www.dare2share.org/store.

Never stop PERSUADING. I know the word "persuading" can have almost a negative sound to it. But I like to think of it as letting our friends know what they are missing. If I was about to do something really dumb (which is not too far fetched to believe), I would hope you would try and "persuade" me not to. You wouldn't have to tell me what I was about to do was dumb. But you could "persuade" me in a loving way that there are far better things to do, things that are more exciting and you could even invite me to try one of those things. That's persuading.

This is really just the beginning. If someone becomes a believer, then you have a Grom to train. Share with them all you have learned about a relationship with Jesus. Invite them to youth group with you or maybe start a Bible study with them once a week. You could give them a copy of this book and you could talk about what you learn in each chapter. As they grow in their understanding of the life they have in Jesus, challenge them to go "all in" by telling their friends about their new life in Jesus. Encourage them to find a Grom. Most importantly, remind them often that it is all about Jesus.

This is how we live "THE Cause."

CHAPTER 15

IN

ZANE

I hope you have enjoyed these crazy "InZane" stories. As I reflect on all that God has done and is doing in my life, I am amazed and it gets me so stoked about what He might do next. What gets me even more stoked is to think about the possibilities of what could happen if each of you reading this book grasped the reality that the God of this Universe lives inside of you.

Think about it. It is absolutely crazy that I am even writing a book. I am an ex-drug dealer who previously drove semi-trucks for a beer company. I got held back in school because I couldn't read! There is nothing that qualifies me to write a book. If there has been anything you have read that has helped you, encouraged you, challenged you, then let it be evidence for the fact that God can use anybody.

It reminds me of something my buddy Greg pointed out to me one day about the potential of teenagers to change the world. There is a story in Matthew 17:24-27, where Jesus seems to be hanging out with all 12 of His disciples. As they approach the temple, they are asked to pay the temple tax. But the crazy part is, only Jesus and Peter pay the temple tax. If you do some Bible leg work and trace back the origins of the temple tax, you'll learn that it all started with the tabernacle tax, described in Exodus 30:14. There you discover that only people 20 years old and older had to pay the tax. So it's significant that in this story in Matthew 17, only Jesus and Peter pay the temple tax. If I'm reading the story right, then only Jesus and Peter were over the age of 20. Which makes the rest of the disciples teenagers.

And it was that group of teenager followers of Jesus who God used to change the world. Teenagers who were empowered by the Spirit of God living in them and who were just crazy enough to believe it was true and pass it on to others.

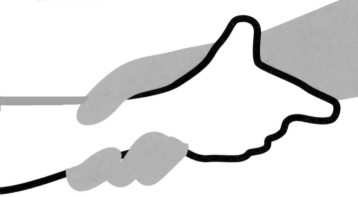

And what's true for them is also true for you. Your potential is not related to how smart you are, how good you are at sports or how popular you are. As Christians, we are not limited to our own abilities. We have been given the very Spirit of God who lives in us and is able to accomplish through us what we could never do on our own. I believe that God has planned for you things that you could never imagine yourself doing. Things way beyond your own capabilities.

That is the real intention of this book. It really isn't meant to be about my life and accomplishments. This book is intended to be more than just about me, it's really meant to be about the One who is "In" Zane. And the same One who is "In" Zane is "In" You, if you are a believer.

God doesn't call the qualified, He qualifies the called.

He doesn't need the able, just the willing.

God is sending you on a mission and you are equipped with His power.

So Go! Unleash the power that is within you. Get stoked on Jesus and let that stoke overflow to your friends.

They need what you have. And God has given you a story, too, and your story is unique. I have told you my story and now it is time to tell your story.

The same God who lives "In" Zane is alive and well "In" You. You need nothing more and you should enjoy nothing less. Imagine the possibilities of all that God could do in and through you. Now live it, so that the world may see that Jesus Christ, though crucified on a cross 2,000 years ago, is actually still alive. And He is displaying His love, power and grace through you.

Christ "IN" You.

Imagine what it would be like if we lived out of this reality and began to look at the challenges in front of us as opportunities. Opportunities for God to do something amazing. I have hopes of seeing every person come to know Jesus and experience freedom, love and life in Him. I can get discouraged by the fact that the world is so big and by just how unlikely it is that I can even make a difference. Or I can chose to do my part, no matter how insignificant I think it to be. Today I am doing my part by writing this book. Sure, maybe you are the only person who will ever read it. But, it is worth it. You are worth it, even if it was just for you. I would do it all over again.

What is your part?

Do you know that there are over 67,000 junior high, middle school and high school campuses across the U.S.? Many of them are full of students who don't know Jesus. That is a lot of schools and it seems impossible to me to reach them all. But what if you did your part and reached

In Zane

out to the students at your school? And what if other students did their part?

Did you know that there is already an army of students uniting together to reach their campuses with the life changing message of Jesus? An army of teenager whose weapons consist of love, compassion, hope and forgiveness, and who are empowered by Jesus Himself living in them.

Will you join this movement?

Log on to www.everyschool.com and adopt your school. You might find that you are not alone. We need your help.

Then go to www.dare2share.org/thecause and get the tools, watch the podcasts and join the online community!

Imagine what it could look like if there were students on every single school campus across America sharing the

143

love of Jesus with their peers. I wonder what it would have looked like if that had happened at my school? Do you know that never once in my entire junior high or high school experience did any student ever tell me about Jesus? What if someone would have been bold enough to reach out to me? How would my life have been different?

There are students just like me walking through the halls of your school and I am begging you, don't let them wander aimlessly through life any longer. You have the message of life, the answers to many of their questions and healing for their hurt. God has empowered you through the presence of His Spirit in you, don't just keep it to yourself, let it out.

I LOOOOOOOOOVE
JESUS!

Prologue

God has absolutely blown me away by all that He has done.
God has moved like wildfire in my friends and family, as
He has used me to spread the message of His love. I am
absolutely amazed at the work that He has done in my
life and in the lives of those around me. I have had the
opportunity to see many of my family members come to love
Jesus and God has used me as part of that process.

Since I became a Christian my dad and I have grown closer
than we ever were before. My dad has become a man who
desires to live his life for Jesus and he has even helped me
with much of this book.

My mom has gone from an every-once-in-awhile church goer
to a committed follower of Jesus. She and I share sermons
and books all the time. She has been one of my biggest
prayer warriors as I have had opportunities to share God's
love with students around the United States.

My (x)-step mom, who I used to not get along with is now like a best friend. God has done an amazing work in her life and she is like a shining beacon of God's grace to those around her. My wife and I go visit her often. Recently she asked if I would baptize her and her husband.

My half sister who is eight years younger than me has stuck by me through everything. She has seen her big brother do some stupid stuff and has always been there for me. After I moved to Bible School, she came out and lived with me for awhile. During that time, God did amazing things in her life. She has since moved back home and continues to share Jesus with her friends.

My other (x)step mom who I didn't write about in this part of my story has had an amazing journey, as well. She and I would stay up late into the night talking about God. She could never accept the fact that there could be just one God. But she is now living for Jesus and works extensively with homeless men and women in the Seattle area.

The friend who was there when I almost drank myself to death continued in the wild life after I left for Bible School. Years later, I had the opportunity to pray together with him as he, too, decided to "take a stand." He has since helped out at some of the youth conferences I have spoke at, even though there have been a couple times I had to vouch for him because the conference didn't allow volunteers to have criminal records.

When I first became a believer, I declared that I was going to be a "bachelor till the rapture." I was convinced that marriage didn't work, so I was going to be single forever. After six years of being a Christian, I met Rachel, the most amazing girl in the world. She loves Jesus and challenges me to do the same. So we got married. Now we live THE Cause together at the Torchbearer Bible School in Winter Park, Colorado, where we get to mentor college age students nine months of the year.

I hope you hear that this truly is not a testimony about me, Zane, but about the one who is "In" Zane. If you are a believer, then this is true about you, too. May you believe that reality and never settle for anything less.

Ephesians 3:20,21 says, "*Now to Him who is able to do immeasurably more than all we ask or imagine according to His POWER that is at work within us, to Him be glory.*"

Zane Slang

chillin' *slang* **1**: in the state of just being **2**: having to do with relaxing **3**: also used for trying to sound like you are fun to be around, when truly you are just bored
Sentence usage: "What did you do this weekend?" "Awe, I was just chillin'."
Word advisory: which really means I did absolutely nothing, but sit on the couch and pick buggers; not usually used as a gauge of temperature, although this is still sometimes acceptable

dece *slang* : short for decent, however does not have the same meaning, having more to do with something of quality
Sentence usage: "Can you believe that dude just threw a quadruple back flip?" "Dude, that was dece."

epic *slang* **1**: referring to something in a positive way **2**: showing that something is amazing
Sentence usage: "That was an epic day of epic riding with an epic ending. It was soooo epic."
Word advisory: many believe this word is overused

hook up *slang* **1**: to provide someone with some sort of item or good, particularly having to do with an illegal substance **2**: also can be used to refer to when a boy and girl start going out
Sentence usage: **1**: "Thanks, hommie, for the hook up on the new stamp collection." **2**: "Did you hear that Alfred and Gertrude hooked up?"
Word advisory: not having to do with placing a plant on a hanger

ill *slang* **1**: refers to something that is cool or neat **2**: can also refer to an experience of something that is enjoyable.
Sentence usage: "That Tupperware party was ill last night."
Word advisory: no longer refers to having a sickness

legit *slang* **1**: short for legitimate **2**: having to do with something being cool
Sentence usage: "Those suspenders are pretty legit, Grandpa."
Word advisory: replaces the word neat, as in "Snowboarding is pretty neat"; may soon be replaced by the word "official"

thanks to Rob and Big; no longer associated with Mc Hammer 2 Legit to Quit

ripper *slang* : someone who has the ability to accomplish difficult tricks on a snowboard or other board sport
Sentence usage: "That kid is such a little ripper, too bad it's only a video game and he can't actually ride."
Word advisory: not used in relation to torn fabric

shred *slang* **1:** To perform well in some type of board sport activity **2:** also can refer to the act of playing an instrument with great speed
Sentence usage: **1:** "Not only can that kid shred a half pipe, he also has a neat stamp collection. **2:** "That guy on the flute sure did shred when it came time for his solo."
Word advisory: probably better used in context of a guitar; not having to do with cheese.
Derivative terminology:
-Shreddin : the act of performing board sports well
-Shredder : one who does perform well at board sports, particularly as a snowboarder

sick *slang* **1:** of or pertaining to amazing, outstanding, excellent. **2:** often used to speak of something in a positive way
Sentence usage: "That game of Pokemon was so sick!"
Word advisory: no longer having to do with having a cold or being disgusting

stoked *slang* : to be very excited, even exhilarated, about something
Sentence usage: "I happen to be very stoked about this formal meeting."
Word advisory: does not usually refer to, but can still be used in reference to keeping a fire going

word *slang* **1**: to be in agreement upon **2**: to compliment for something well said **3**: an acknowledgement for something stated **4**: also used as a greeting **5**: also can be used in reference to the Bible and even being in ultimate agreement with it
Sentence usage: "That musical last night was legit." "Word."
Word advisory: not just letters compiled together communicating meaning

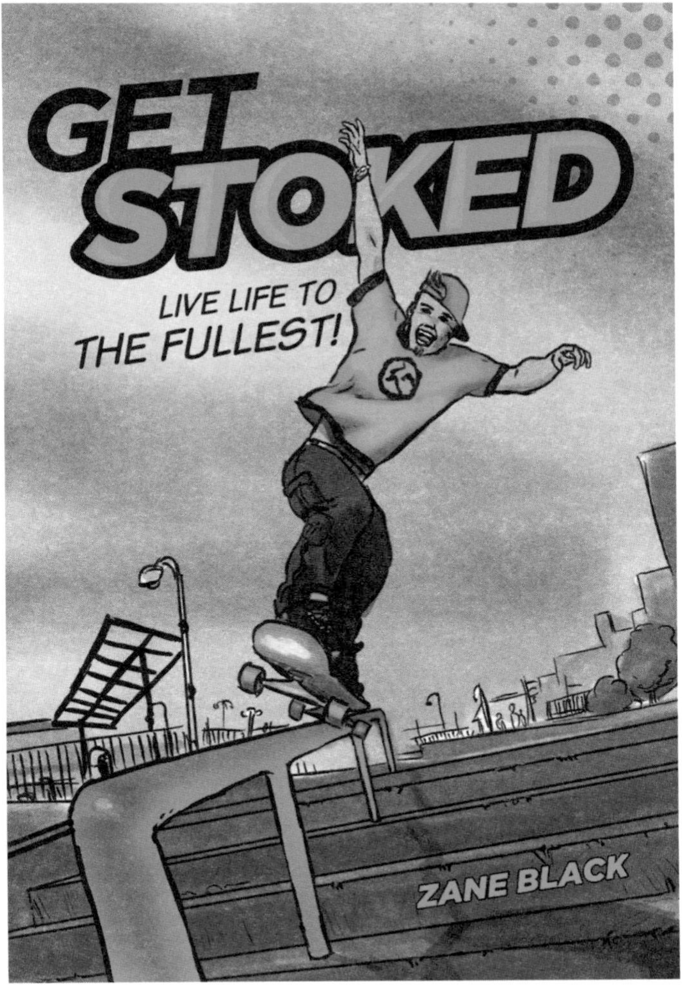
GET STOKED
LIVE LIFE TO THE FULLEST!
ZANE BLACK

Hey, I'm Zane,

which probably means nothing to you, and that's okay. I'm assuming a friend gave this to you because they thought hearing my story might help you out some. Or maybe you were stuck in the woods and had "to go" and this was the only thing you could find to use as paper. But for some reason you decided to read before you wiped. Awesome.

Anyway, here's my story...

I barely graduate, squeaking by thanks to a principal who lets some things slide so he won't have to deal with me for another year.

But the reality I discover is that it just isn't all it's cracked up to be. Sure it's fun, but that type of fun only lasts for a while. When the fun ends (and it eventually will), along come the consequences and side effects that are never anticipated.

It's like jumping off a 100 story building. It would be fun for awhile. Until you encounter the reality of the pavement. Just because something is fun for awhile doesn't mean it is a good decision. We have to look beyond the moment, and factor in the hard reality of the quickly approaching side effects.

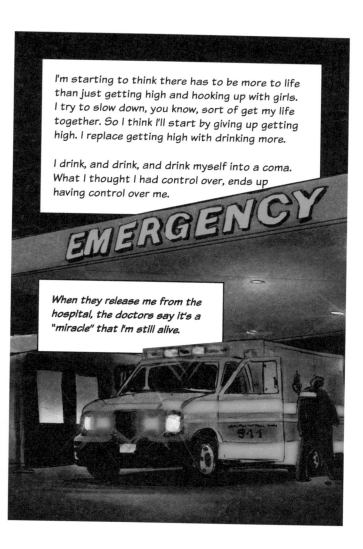

But it's only a matter of days before I'm back at it. Drinking, drugs and all the stuff that goes along with it. Slowly I begin to realize this is no way to live my life. I want to experience all that life has to offer, but in the quest for fullness of life, I almost just lost my life. *What now? I feel like there's no way out.*

Maybe you've had similar feelings. Maybe you've felt like life isn't what you want it to be, maybe you've made mistakes, maybe you've just felt like there has got to be more to life or maybe some horrible things have happened to you that aren't your fault.

I want you to know there is more to life, there is a way out, there is freedom from your past and healing for your hurt.

I finally hear about the real Jesus. Now I know most all of us have at least heard about Jesus. I mean in America we celebrate His birthday (Christmas) and we are the ones who get the presents, which is a pretty sweet deal. But at that church I hear about Jesus in a way that I have never heard before. They talk about Jesus as if He is the most important thing in their lives. It isn't about a list of rules, but about getting to know the God who we were made to be in relationship with.

Just as a snowboard is made to be ridden on the snow, we are made to be in relationship with God. Sure, I've ridden my snowboard down some sand dunes, behind a boat and even towed behind a car on wet grass. All of those times having a ton of fun, but it is not what the snowboard is made for. None of those compare to using the snowboard for what it was made for, the SNOW!

Same with life. We are made to be in relationship with Jesus. When we don't live our life for the purpose it is designed, we are missing out on life to the fullest.

But because of the selfish things we've done, we've been separated from that relationship. Those things are called "sin," everything from telling a lie to murdering someone. The Bible says that if we've done one little thing wrong, we are guilty—we fall short of God's perfect standard, creating a chasm between us and a perfect God.

So no matter what you have or haven't done, we are all in the same boat, we are sinners. We are born with that selfish nature, which is why you never have to teach a toddler to be selfish, it's in their nature.

The Bible says that our sins cannot be removed by good deeds, meaning there's nothing we can do to wipe away the bad things we've done and get back to God.

But this is why Jesus died on the cross, to take the penalty for our sins and bridge the chasm for us.

But the story doesn't end with Jesus dead. Three days later He rose from the dead to new life and He now offers His life to each and every one of us.

When I first hear this message, I have a lot of doubts and a lot of questions. But I know the way I'm living isn't working and that I'm missing something.

Could this be what you are missing, too?

I make a choice to give it a shot, to take a chance. I decide to believe in Jesus and what He did on the cross. I begin to trust Jesus to be the one who "saves" me from the penalty for my sin and gives me new life now.

Jesus wants to give us life, and life to the fullest! This is what I'm looking for. I want to experience the fullness of this life. Do you? Is there anything holding you back from believing in Jesus and trusting Him for this life right now?

Becoming a believer and a follower of Jesus is the greatest thing in my entire life. Please don't get me wrong, it isn't always easy and things don't always go my way. But in the midst of life, even the hard times, I've found a joy that no one is able to take away, a fullness that nothing else compares to and a whole new purpose for my life here on earth. I want everyone to experience this joy that Jesus brings.

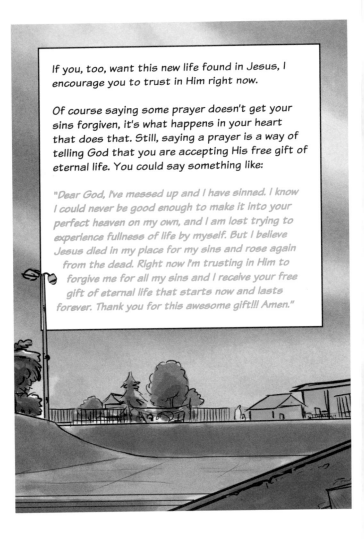

If you, too, want this new life found in Jesus, I encourage you to trust in Him right now.

Of course saying some prayer doesn't get your sins forgiven, it's what happens in your heart that does that. Still, saying a prayer is a way of telling God that you are accepting His free gift of eternal life. You could say something like:

"Dear God, I've messed up and I have sinned. I know I could never be good enough to make it into your perfect heaven on my own, and I am lost trying to experience fullness of life by myself. But I believe Jesus died in my place for my sins and rose again from the dead. Right now I'm trusting in Him to forgive me for all my sins and I receive your free gift of eternal life that starts now and lasts forever. Thank you for this awesome gift!!! Amen."

Now I can't stop telling people about this new life in Jesus. That is why I wrote this. I would love to hear your thoughts or questions, whether this helped you in any way or even if you just left it with the pile of "stuff" in the woods. zaneblack.com.

For more information about what it means to experience all that Jesus has for you, talk to the friend who gave you this or go to gospeljourney.com.

If you aren't like totally offended or mad at me and would love to know more, you could also check out my book *InZane* to hear more of my story and more importantly, more of Jesus' story. If you made a decision to put your faith and trust in Jesus, talk to your friend who gave you this and they will help you grow in your new relationship with Him so you can live life to the fullest!